Twelve Grindstones

Twelve Grindstones

*or, A Few More Good Ones, being another
cultural roundup of Maine folklore, sort of,
although not intended to be definitive,
and perhaps not so cultural, either,*

by John Gould

Illustrations by Edward Malsberg

Little, Brown and Company   Boston   Toronto

LIBRARY OF CONGRESS CATALOG CARD NO. 76–105352

FIRST EDITION

*Published simultaneously in Canada
by Little, Brown & Company (Canada) Limited*

PRINTED IN THE UNITED STATES OF AMERICA

For Julie
(of course!)

Twelve Grindstones

Blueberry Plucker

The great, if merited, success of my scholarly exegesis on Maine folklore (*The Jonesport Raffle,* Little, Brown, 1969) suggests that further studies may be amusing and profitable. The whole matter is like dipping the ocean dry with a spoon. The particular advantage I have in this field of academic research is that I am privy to how it works. The visiting professional scholar, delving into Maine folklore methodically, must isolate his instances individually — coming up with one now and another later. Being to the manner born, so to speak, I have the advantage of multiple access. For me there is no such thing as an isolated example. My kind are like blueberries on the bush — whole handfuls may be swept off at once.

Nor must I approach and establish myself, head on. I slip in. For instance, I find Joe and Charley and Jim leaning over the wire looking at Jim's new coonhound, and as I come up and lean with them I do not have to say, "Pardon me, gentlemen, but I am a doctor of philosophy from Tulane University and I am investigating the incidence of down-east folklore — would you care to say a few words into this electronic recording device?"

My approach, although equally erudite, is more casual. I lean, and before they get a chance to say anything I remark, "Did you hear about the fellow who sat up all night studying for his urine test?"

(This, we scholars have pigeonholed as the Polish Joke. It must be handled carefully in this age of integration and brotherly affection, for literature as well as politics is flunky to the Supreme Court. In Providence, Rhode Island, the Polish Joke becomes the Italian Joke. In Maine, it is usually the French-Canadian Joke. The script is the same in any language. The gist, pretty much, is that it takes five men to replace an electric light bulb — one to hold the bulb and four to turn the stepladder. However, in Maine there are often combinations which show the originality of the people and may be termed crossbreeds. Such as:

What is this?

Xski
X

(This is a Frenchman cosigning a note with a Polack.)

So, having broached a general topic with Joe, Charley, and Jim, and the research area established, I now have things going for me that a Tulane professor wouldn't understand, and my doctoral work is merely to listen and remember.

"No," says Charley. "But I heard about the fellow

who got a pair of water skis and drove all over Maine looking for a pond with a hill on it."

Joe says, "Last Saturday a fellow telephoned my garage and told me to come over and get his car unlocked — he left the keys inside. I said I'd be over in a few minutes, and he said to hurry up because he had a convertible with the top down and it looked like rain."

Jim said, "He must have been a relative of that fellow who bought a chain saw and cut five cords of wood with it the first afternoon. He was so pleased with it they decided to show him how to start the motor."

This is quite enough scholastic research for one day, so now I can give over the cultural badinage and revert to my honest role as friend, neighbor, accessory, and accomplice. "That dog don't look overbright, either," I say.

"He ain't," says Jim.

Joe says, "He claims he can play cribbage, but I beat him two games out of three."

"I take it he's a coonhound," I say.

"Eyah," says Jim. "And a foxhound and a rabbit-hound and a cathound and a skunkhound and a hen-hound and I don't know what-all. He dug out a mole this morning. He's like the Kennedys — he's got to take on everything. I suppose you're standing there looking at the most well-rounded dog in the world, and he ain't worth a hole in the snow."

"How do you happen to possess such a creature?" I ask.

"I just this minute gave him to you."

"What would I want him for?"

"You can go into business and make your own dog manure."

This colloquy will suffice to demonstrate the difference between formal academic pursuit of the elusive folklore and the manner in which it is researched in its native lair by one familiar with its habits. It also shows that a single foray (see *The Jonesport Raffle*) doesn't exhaust the chances. Now that I have become a serious student of folklore, thanks to the vast profits that continue to roll in, I find I work no more than an hour or two a day. This leaves ample time for rest, refreshment, and the management of my philanthropies. But the State of Maine, the nesting place of the true species, is busy twenty-four hours a day, the clock around, year in and year out, creating, refining, and embellishing folklore. I, or any other researchist, will never catch up.

Home to Roost

In the long ago the United States mails were handled mostly by the Railway Post Offices, and a whole grid of RPO's operated the length and breadth of Maine. Most of them were short runs with but one or two clerks riding in the car to sort mail in transit and to take in and put off bags when the train stopped. Those trains were work trains, handling freight, mail, baggage, and passengers, and stopping at every small town on the line. But each mail car was in fact a rolling post office and had all the status of any municipal mail center — it sold stamps and money orders, kept a cancellation stamp, and had a slot on the side for dropping letters. The big post office in Portland was no more a post office than the mail car that rolled up to Rumford and was called the Rumford & Portland RPO — distilled in the lingo of the railway postal clerks to Rum & Port.

But the major RPO in Maine was on the through line, and of all the mail cars on the Vanceboro & Boston RPO the elite were the sixty-footers that howled through the night on the Maritime Express. This was one of the continent's great trains, and for a long time maintained the fastest over-the-route speed of all. It made up more or less simultaneously on each end, and as the eastbound pulled out of North Station in Boston, its westbound counterpart would leave Halifax. Boston has always had close affinity with the Maritimes, and as relatives visited back and forth the Maritime Express accommodated them and showed a profit for the Boston & Maine, the Maine Central, the Canadian Pacific, and the Canadian National — all joining in the operation. Many a night the train would run in two sections — mail and express cars first, and the sleepers and coaches following close behind. Even in the early days of its run the train averaged something like eighty miles an hour, and on the level stretches of Maine's Sebasticook Valley it would throttle up and clock off an even hundred for mile after mile. It was a friendly train, where folks from "down east" socialized and shared sandwiches. Those who didn't take a sleeper would curl up on a seat, and if their overcoat coverlet slipped off, a brakeman would smooth it back. To those leaving Boston for the Maritime homeland, the first stop of consequence was Mac-Adam Junction for breakfast — a thirty-minute pause just after daybreak. Here the Canadian National took over. For those coming to Boston the night was a rolling, jolting charge down the wilderness corridors of Maine to arrive at North Station about seven o'clock — just before the morning rush of suburban commuter trains. Clearly, to be a railway postal clerk on the Maritime Express was top-hole.

For people asleep, the few stops across Maine were only silent pauses in the roar of the wheels, but to the postal clerks, Biddeford, Portland, Waterville, and Bangor were busy spots. Here they exchanged incoming for outgoing pouches, rearranged their stacks of bags, and closed the doors to make ready for the next town. And that meant the next town, because the Maritime Express pouched whether it stopped or not. As the train roared through a sleeping community a bag would be kicked from the mail car door into the night, to be picked up by a waiting mail messenger, and then a hook would be pulled up to snag a bag hanging on a trackside yardarm. Throwing and catching was a delicate maneuver, and a new clerk, or one who wasn't paying attention, could sometimes heave a bag into the river, or a greenhouse, and then see the hanging pouch rush by before he got the hook up.

Newport was in the Sebasticook Valley, and still is. When the engineer advanced the throttle up to an even century, the great train of fifteen or eighteen cars would go through Newport like a bullet going past a knothole. Throwing and catching at Newport would have been fraught with continuing surprises, except that the engineer always hit his precise hundred, and held it. This gave the postal clerks a delicate advantage. The pouch was supposed to land on a patch of green grass, or in winter in the snowbank that covered it, between the water tank and the freight shed. Too soon, or too late — disaster. They would lay the pouch in the car door and listen for the click of a certain yard switch. Then, instantly, a switchman's shanty lantern would flick past. Taking the count from there a clerk would tell off nine seconds on his watch, and at nine they would place-kick the pouch into the Newport night. It would land exactly on the little patch of green grass. If the engineer hadn't been in cahoots and the train hadn't sustained its speed, the pouch could have ended up in many an interesting place.

Now, during World War I butter was hard to come by. It was on ration stamps if you could find any, and the price was high. But one of the postal clerks in the crew on the Maritime Express lived near Newport, and his daily "run" started from that station. He would work down to Portland on a day train, join the Maritime Express as far as Bangor, and then work back to Newport on a local. That was his day's work. And one night he said, "Hell, I can get you all the butter you want. The station agent at Newport has a brother who keeps cows — they make butter all the time. How much do you want?"

So this man took two pounds, and another took five, and when they added up the total demand it came to thirty-three pounds. "Sure," he said. "I'll pick up thirty-three pounds and bring it on the next trip."

So he did. He came on the train at Portland with a big bundle done up in brown paper, and after the pouches were hung and the work under way he undid the brown wrapper and began to give each clerk his requested amount. But the mail car was inundated with a loud and smothering stench. The butter was more than strong — it was rancid. It had the appearance of being rancid a long time. He quickly wrapped up the bundle again and tied the string with a double knot. He kicked the thirty-three pounds of butter under a sorting case, which is a poor place for butter. Mail cars always rode in the position of honor, next behind the locomotive, and this gave them first crack at the steam heat. As the Maritime Express hurtled through the Maine night the butter thus became more rugged, although softer, and the stench was unbearable even to the clerk in the far end of the car who was sorting mail for Prince Edward Island. Many a sharp opinion was expressed about the parentage of the station agent at Newport and his brother who kept a few cows.

And then one of the clerks who had been watching the time said, "Get ready for Newport," and they opened the car door. They listened for the switch, and they saw the fleeting flash of the switchman's shanty lantern. They counted off nine seconds — and then they counted ten, eleven, and twelve. At twelve, they place-kicked the thirty-three pounds of butter from the threshold. And they closed the door.

The brown paper bundle hit the side of the Newport depot at a westbound, or ricochet, spot, and the station agent who had a brother who kept cows was providentially positioned on the platform, watch in hand, to see the train go by. He got most of it, but thirty-three pounds is a lot of butter and when strong and rancid, butter will go much farther. Newport was largely a mess.

The moral is that when you butter somebody up, it's a lot more fun at 100 mph.

How to Buy Wood

Old Henry had been a clerk in the Osgood Store for years, and one day a man came in and asked for Old Henry. Mr. Osgood said, "Why, Henry died last week."

"I'm sorry to hear that," said the man. And, after a pause, "Then there must be a vacancy?"

"No," said Mr. Osgood. "Henry didn't leave no vacancy."

A farm housewife known for her stingy portions at dinner, whenever she couldn't avoid feeding somebody, was occasionally twitted about it in sly remarks by those at her table. Once, with hot biscuits, she served a guest a remarkably small portion of comb honey. He surveyed it and said, "Aha! I see you keep a bee."

In Washington County Superior Court some terms ago, the justice was asking a few questions of the defendant in a divorce action. He said, "Have you been faithful to your wife?"

The gentleman replied, "Oh, yes — frequently."

Roland Baker had guided in the Rangeley Lakes region for years, and one of his regular "sports" was a wealthy New Yorker who always said farewell with, "And if you get down to New York this winter, be sure and look me up!" So one winter Roland was in New York for the sportsmen's show, and he looked the man up. He found the place, sounded the gong, and was royally received. Hospitality was complete and Roland had one of the best times of his life. After he got back to Rangeley he liked to tell about it, and a portion of his story went like this:

". . . and then before we went in to eat supper, they come around with some horse's doovers — that's French for eating between meals."

Flint Johnson's wife tells about the little girl from St. Come, up in Quebec, who came down to Maine to work in a summer camp. She spoke no English, and nobody in camp spoke any French, so Mrs. Johnson surmised the young lady might be lonesome. But then she heard the girl was making out fine, as the guides had undertaken to teach her some English. Soon afterwards Mrs. Johnson saw the girl in Riddle's Drug Store, so she spoke to her and said, "How's your English coming along?"

The girl said, "Goddam good!"

Roy Davis tells about the farmer in Newry who built a new shed, and he put a small and untrustworthy padlock on the door. "That lock won't do any good," somebody said to him.

"Well, it'll keep honest people from stealing."

The town of Harmony once claimed the biggest skinflint in the state. He came into Benoit's store one day with an egg in his hand and said, "My wife needs a new darning needle — will you swap me one for this egg?"

Benoit well knew the old fellow's reputation so, amused, he said, "Oh, I suppose so," and they went to the dry goods section in the rear of the store to select the needle. As they walked back to the front of the store Benoit had the egg in his hand, and the skinflint said, "Oh, I see you've put in a new sody fountain!"

Benoit said, "Yes, they're becoming popular, and I thought I'd give one a whirl."

"Well," said the old fellow, "don't that call for a drink on the house?"

"Sure," said Benoit. "What'll you have?"

"Anything with an egg in it."

So Benoit broke the egg in a glass, and it turned out to be a double-yolker.

"Aha!" said the skinflint. "You owe me another needle!"

A. W. Plummer, M.D., used to tell about the time he was driving out in the country to make a call, and he noticed the roof on a farmhouse had burst into flame around the chimney. He turned his horse into the driveway, pounded on the door, and when a woman stuck her head out he said, "Your house is on fire!"

Whether she was preoccupied or stupid, or perhaps didn't understand, the doctor never knew, but she said, "Is that all?"

Dr. Plummer said, "Well, that's all I happen to think of at the moment."

In Kennebec County Court they once had a case of accidental shooting — a hunting affair which may or may not have been quite that accidental. As in most cases of this kind arising out of the fall demises, both state and defense were moving cautiously, the one not caring to accuse where the other was loath to defend, and vice versa, and inferences were heaped on implications until the story got very interesting. At one point the defendant was telling his version of what happened, and he said that he mistook the victim for a deer.

Absorbed in the tale, His Honor leaned down over the bench and said, "Buck or doe?"

Elected to the city council in Lewiston, a man of low social order, no education, and nothing else to qualify him except that he got the most votes, was eager to take part in his first session. So when the city treasurer reported a deficit he cried out, "Let's spend it!"

Virgil Rodney lost an arm in some engagement in the Spanish-American War and had a lot of fun over it the rest of his life. Somebody was always coming up to sympathize and inquire as to how he lost it. Rodney would say, "Now, a good many people ask me that, and the truth is that it always embarrasses me. So I have made a rule, and I'll tell you how I lost my arm if you'll promise not to ask me any more questions about it."

"Certainly."

"Well," says Virgil, "it was bit off."

In town meeting at Freeport the citizens were voting on the school budget, and came to "Physical Training." In those days this was a new idea, and it had been voted through the year before on a trial basis. Most of the objection was in this vein: "I'll give my young-uns exercise enough splittin' wood, they don't need no teacher for working up a sweat." But the educators deemed the subject important, and the citizens went along. A graduate of Sargent School, a young lady, was hired to conduct the classes — she coached girls' basketball, and otherwise instructed in the care of the teeth, keeping the scalp clean, and related delicate topics. Now, after a year's trial, most citizens seemed to be "agin" it, but surprisingly one old farmer took the floor and supported the idea.

"I'm in favor of it," he said, "and I'll tell you why. We got a bunch of kids at our place, and while we try to bring them up right and be decent parents, I got to admit there are times when we fall short. Like, you take, brushing teeth. We keep after them, and we do what we can, but it ain't the same. We never had no luck keeping them faithful at it. But they've had a year of this here physical training, and they like the teacher first-rate, and now when they get up in the morning they fight for the toothbrush."

Judge William R. Pattangall once defended a man accused of arson. This fellow closed his home in Machias and started for Florida to spend the winter. Police intercepted him somewhere in South Carolina, told him his house had burned down, and held him for the Maine authorities. The state contended he had lighted a candle in a basket of shavings, and when it burned down it set his house afire. Judge Pattangall, who had not been elevated at that time and was merely a practicing attorney, made his usual dramatic and effective appearance, and rather easily got the man acquitted.

The next day the man came into Pattangall's office to pay his fee, and with his departing handshake he said, "Now, Bill, if there's ever anything I can do for you, don't hesitate to call on."

"Well," said Pattangall. "There is something you can do for me. I wish you'd tell me where in hell you got a candle that would burn for three days."

Although Pattangall is better remembered for his trials, his career as a judge was not without the Pattangall touch. A juror, one time, asked to be excused and for his reason said, "My wife is about to become pregnant."

"Excused!" said the judge, instantly.

At this, one of the lawyers said, "I'm sure the court understands that the man means that his wife is about to be delivered of a child."

"Still excused," said Judge Pattangall. "This court recognizes both emergencies."

Del Bates tells about the fellow who came down from Patten to represent that town in the state legislature, and he was so horrified at the runaway tendencies that he began voting no on every appropriation. Early in the session this didn't matter, but later his vote became critical on a number of issues and quite an effort was made to switch him. But he remained adamant, so the party leaders finally asked the governor to intervene.

The fellow was impressed to be invited into the "front office" and he found the governor affable. But even with this high-quality coaxing he refused to change his vote. "I'm sure," said the governor at last, "that there must be a good many men in Patten more sensible than you are that the good people there could have sent down to represent them."

"There are," he said. "Any number of them. But I'm the only one who had a suit of clothes."

And now: how to buy wood. When the old Pejepscot Paper Company decided to liquidate its upriver pulp mill, it was soon picked up by the U.S. Gypsum Company, who began making wood-pulp insulation board. It was a good item and has proved a popular and profitable product. This is the only mill that widespread company has in Maine, and the sudden confrontation of Chicago management and Maine operation created some exciting times. For one thing, somebody had to come from the home office to inspect all departments and operations, so the directors would be informed as they programmed this new mill. When this vice-president arrived, full of big ideas, he had the best intentions in the world, but he was a nuisance. Everybody was polite, but nobody knew just how to deal with him. He was referred to as "The Snoop," and his questions were courteously answered even if they were sometimes foolish. In time he had inspected everything except the buying of wood.

Wood buying is difficult to explain. No forest based mill can operate without wood, and since U.S. Gypsum was new to Maine and owned no timberlands, they depended on buying in the open market Some mills own and operate their own timberlands. Some own, but contract for the cutting. Some don't own much land, but have *entrepreneurs de bois* who look after their interests. Some mills with surplus wood sell to other mills. Some mills use spruce but no pine, and so on. But no matter how the wood is grown and acquired, the mill can't operate without it, and the wood buyer is the key man in the whole operation. Brice Booker was the wood buyer for U.S. Gypsum, and in a competitive and far-flung field he was getting all the wood they needed at favorable prices. And one day the vice-president from Chicago came to Brice and said he had inspected everything else and he was now ready to give his attention to the wood-buying department. Brice had heard about the nuisance this fellow had been all through the mill, and he hadn't been looking forward happily to this moment.

"Well, I tell you," said Brice. "Wood buying is kind of an involved matter, and it doesn't have any set location. I keep a desk here in the mill, but sometimes I don't sit at it for a month. I think the best way to handle this is for you to just report that everything is well in hand."

"No," said the vice-president. "I'm obliged to go deeper than that. I want to see how wood is acquired, and I need to know the secrets of an adequate wood supply."

The last thing in the world Brice Booker wanted was to have anybody learn his secrets, because they were exactly what made him the best wood buyer for miles around, but he was stuck with the fellow, so he says, "All right — where are you staying?"

"I'm at the Eagle Hotel in Brunswick."

"Good," says Brice. "Tomorrow morning you be ready at six o'clock, and I'll pick you up and we'll go buy some wood."

The old Eagle Hotel hadn't seen a vice-president that early in the morning, ever, but they had the fellow on the doorstep when Brice drove up. Away they went, and Brice drove without stopping until he came to the town of Guilford, which is pretty-nigh up to Moosehead Lake, in Piscataquis County. He pulled up before a little, shingled office building with a false front, on which a sign said: HORACE MASON, ATTORNEY-AT-LAW, REAL ESTATE & INSURANCE, FORESTER & SURVEYOR, NOTARY PUBLIC.

"Here we are," said Brice, and they went in to find a man poking the fire in a potbelly stove. He turned to see who was coming in, and was clearly delighted to see Brice.

After the handshake and "How's the family," Brice said, "Oh, I want you to meet a vice-president of my company."

Then Brice said, "I've been wondering — did you have any luck moving that old theatre building?"

Squire Mason said, "Yes, I did. Fellow from Bangor. Got my money, and he seems happy."

"Good," said Brice. "I've been worried about you on that deal."

"No need to," said the squire. "I made out."

Then there was a little more small talk, and Brice jumped up and said, "Well, we got to be pushing along. Awful good to see you. Shun evil companions!" and he started for the door. And he contrived to let the vice-president go out through the door first, so the vice-president never heard the rest of the conversation, which went like this:

Booker — You going to have some wood for me this season?

Mason — Eyah.

Booker — Good.

Mason — Same amount?

Booker — Eyah.

Mason — Same price?

Booker — Eyah.

Mason — Will do. It's as good as on the cars.

Booker — See ya!

And he shut the door. He got the vice-president in the automobile and drove without stopping back to Brunswick, where he let the vice-president out on the steps of the Eagle Hotel.

"There you are, all safe and sound," said Brice, "and now you've seen how we buy wood."

"Well," said the vice-president. "I've had a pleasant ride, and I've seen a good part of the State of Maine, but I don't see what that trip had to do with buying wood."

"You will," said Brice. "The vouchers will be coming through any day, and you'll see we bought forty-thousand cords at eleven dollars a cord."

The Miracle

The one valid ecclesiastical miracle in Maine folklore naturally has a backwoods theme — stump pulling. This would have no standing at Lourdes and Ste. Anne de Beaupré, or at any sanctified spot where piety and faith have wrought amazing things in more esoteric categories. But to a great throng of people it demonstrated the power of prayer, and because a crowd was on hand there is no need to prove the miracle by assembling great congregations of bishops to assess the evidence. It may well be, accordingly, the only miracle ever brought off before an assemblage. You can dispute forever about the voices St. Joan heard, or what St. Bernadette saw, but when a stump comes out of the ground you've got something you can deal with personally.

The Miracle

Years ago at the Church of St. John the Baptist, which in Maine is correctly spelled Sahnzhahnbateese, the pastor was a Marist named Father André. He was a wiry, graying, little priest with a somewhat fierce visage, not small of stature but hardly medium. Being of Canadian *habitant* origins, he admired the traditions, and was seldom seen, as other priests often were, in trousers. He wore the skirts and dangled his beads. His whole parish was French-Canadian, and as Quebec origins were locally esteemed, Father André was revered. He actually had the quiet wit and good humor of his breed, but he seemed to try diligently to be austere, no doubt for clerical reasons. It was rare to see him smile, but when he did, it was at some gentle phrase, or some mild outcropping of human nature that often indicated his amusement was more worldly than not. He was thoroughly devout, however, and not a priest who sang a mass and then ran down the stairs. Every waking moment was given to his church and his flock, and he put no more piety and love, and no less, into a baptism than he lavished on his mortification of washing down the church steps. He was an unusual priest, and a great man.

That he was not unfamiliar with worldly things was evident when he bought a machine for sorting and counting coins. The stewardship of his parish fretted him, for he had thousands of things he would like to be doing, and his parishioners insisted on silver collections. It was not a poor parish, but it was conservative, and while adequate funds came in, there was little folding money. Counting nickels, dimes, and quarters took time, so Father André bought a banker's machine with a hopper and a crank, and it was expected to be a great help. He screwed it to a table in the sacristy and was cranking at it one day when a candle salesman from Portland walked in unannounced and surprised Father André. At the moment Father André was speaking a few basic *habitant* words which are not in the approved vocabulary of the Society of Mary, and are more often heard in rural Quebec when a horse steps on a man's foot or a cow kicks over a milk pail. Father André was not at all embarrassed, but the salesman didn't know what to do. "This machine," said Father André, "vexes me."

The reason it vexed him was its unilateral nature. It wouldn't count Canadian money, but gummed up every time anything except good United States coins came along. Since his parishioners were visiting back and forth to Canada all the time, they found the church collection plate a good place to work off the odd coins they brought back from *les cantons de l'est*. It was enough to make a priest swear.

But Father André was one who knew that God would always understand, even if candle salesmen mightn't, and he was constantly at work on projects that many another priest might not care to tackle, which is why he bought a stump puller.

Just recently he had purchased, for the parish, a lot of land to enlarge the cemetery. It lay just east of Bowdoin College, all this being in Brunswick, and because the land is sandy through the section it made easy digging for the sexton. The spot sloped up from the highway, and when Father André acquired it the growth was mostly Norway pine. This is an inferior conifer, not much good for lumber and hardly fit for firewood, and by no means suited for arboreal décor in a prosperous cemetery. Father André called for volunteers and all the trees were chopped down — he himself working along with the men, skirts flying and beads askew. An ax is no stranger to a Quebec farm boy. Indeed, his participation made the job short, because every man was trying to get his tree down before the priest got his. Then they had to pull the stumps.

The stump puller Father André bought was a standard item before bulldozers and backhoes, and it worked on a simple principle of leverage. Chains fitted around two stumps and came together with a little handle between them. Father André would work the little handle back and forth and the chains would be taken up, and gradually, one pulling against the other, one of the stumps would come out of the ground. It depended on which stump was the stronger. As the

work of clearing the land progressed, it had ample publicity because Father André was forever enlisting volunteers, and along in the action somewhere somebody
thoughtfully raised the question of how he was going
to pull his last stump. What would he do when he had
nothing to pull against?

When he was asked about this he would indulge in
one of his infrequent smiles, as if he had a little joke
within his heart and nobody knew it but him. He
would say, "Come and see." And that's just what
everybody did. On the afternoon when things were
getting down to the last stump, a crowd showed up
that was by no means limited to the parishioners of the
Church of St. John the Baptist. The whole town came.
Father André arrived in his skirt and carrying a shovel,
and he found more people than had ever crowded into
St. John's for a New Year's midnight mass. And the
little priest was seen to smile — just a little. Then they
unlocked the toolhouse door and got out the stump
puller, and after a couple of pulls they were down to
two stumps. Which would come out and which would
stay? Which was to be the final conundrum? The men
attached the chains. Father André worked the little
handle and took up the slack.

Then he stopped, and as if noticing for the first time,
he surveyed the crowd. He straightened his garment,
arranged his beads, gazed heavenward in a reverent
way, and spoke. He said, "In the name of the Father

and the Son and the Holy Ghost Amen." Even some black protestants who had just come along to see where the crowd was going found themselves involuntarily making the sign of the Cross. Adroitly, as master of his craft, Father André had instantly brought the scene of toil to a spiritual peak. He prayed. It was an ordinary kind of prayer — the sort a clergyman keeps on tap should he be called on to say a few appropriate words. But it was enough to cast the spell. Nobody doubted that God, now, was helping. Father André turned and began working the little handle.

Both stumps came out of the ground at the same time. Neither was stronger; neither was weaker. Slowly, dripping the sand from their roots and rootlets, each stump drew toward the other, with Father André seeming not to notice and his hand still working the lever. One man, who was near him, said he saw the brief smile that Father André allowed to form — but it soon vanished, and nobody else in the whole crowd was smiling, or anything else. People dispersed slowly, walking away silently. It was indeed a miracle. Nobody had ever before seen, or even heard of, two stumps coming out together.

No, the miracle of St. John's Cemetery has had no notice from Rome, nor up to a late hour has Father André been nominated for sanctification. Probably it's the location and subject matter. The State of Maine isn't mystical enough, and there were no voices and visions. You can't get mileage in holy places out of pulling stumps. But it was a good miracle all the same, and those who saw it were impressed.

The Lobster War

Not always can the origins of folklore material be pinpointed, but there is one expression in the lobster fisheries whose beginning is known. The author of this expression was not a lobsterman, or even a State of Mainer — he was Dr. Ernest Gruening, once governor of the Virgin Islands, once governor of Alaska, and Alaska's first senator after statehood. Originally, he was a Boston newspaperman, and in that profession he became a specialist at doctoring sick newspapers. He had a crew of experts and they'd move in on a journal with anemia and for a fee would conduct the therapy. With this crew he was retained by a group of electric power companies to come to Maine in the late 1920's and found a newspaper in Portland — which he did, and it was the *Portland Evening News*.

His crew was more than able — it was talented and versatile, and it had the knack of handling news coverage to excite a readership. Things went well, and in a relatively short time the *News* had an afternoon circulation of some thirty thousand, which is very good in Maine, and it had the people of the state all worked up over the exportation of hydroelectric power — precisely what the *News* had been founded to prevent. Those were the days of Samuel Insull, and there was war in the electricity business. The established Portland papers had clearly embraced the Insull purposes, and Insull's competition was willing to spend a lot of money to counteract this editorial advantage.

The pitch was that if Maine refused to export surplus power it would attract industry into the state, which would be far better than serving as a powerhouse for mills and factories in Massachusetts, and so on. Dr. Gruening was successful, because Maine people in a referendum vote refused to export power. That there was some merit in his argument may possibly be shown by the presence today of the great St. Regis paper mill at Bucksport — which may even have made the sheet you are now reading. This mill was built in 1930 by out-of-state financing, and it was designed almost entirely as an electrically operated plant. It has certainly made Bucksport prosperous, and used up a lot of nonexported kilowatts. Anyway, Dr. Gruening knew his trade, his crew was clever, and while this power question was in contention he gave Maine a very fine newspaper. Afterward, when the referendum was over, Dr. Gruening moved along to rejuvenate the *New York Post*.

But for a time we had an active, alert, dedicated newspaper, edited and written by talent far above the Maine normal, and to gain an audience for its hydropower editorials the *News* had to offer thorough coverage of all Maine's affairs. But with so many imported, non-Maine, staffers, the paper did get into some newcomer binds.

Dr. Gruening was scholarly, and sharp. Since the existing Maine papers had been getting along profitably on a minimum of talent and application, he decided an "up" style would have an advantage. At the time, any one of the Boston newspapers was outselling the combined Maine papers in their own areas, and Dr. Gruening realized that to gain a substantial readership in Maine he must consider Boston his competition, too. Since he had learned his trade on Newspaper Row he was well aware of the Boston philosophies of circulation. Among the things he advanced to develop his policies was his style sheet, which he posted in the editorial chambers for his writers and editors. It was meant to give the readers a little highbrow and impress his public that *News* reporters could spell hard words. One of his rules was that nobody should refer to an automobile as a "car." Thus, the other papers said that cars had been stolen, cars had been wrecked, and that when the drawbridge stuck open, the cars were backed up for four miles. In the *News* these cars became automobiles, motor vehicles, conveyances, and so on — the idea being that if a reporter were meticulous enough to call a car a motor vehicle, he would be equally careful when describing a power failure in Lubec. A power failure proving, of course, that the Insull interests were inefficient.

Just as the electricity war was peaking, Maine came up with another one — a lobster war out around Matinicus. Matinicus Island is a dot in the outer reaches of Penobscot Bay. Not too many people live there, but for those who do, lobstering is the economy, and they are not happy when fishermen from the mainland wander out that way to set a few traps. Every once in a while a lobster war breaks out, and it is a fearful thing. There is no set rule about what starts one. It can begin in Boston where dealers shave prices, or it can begin when somebody monkeys with the wrong wife. In lobstering, no man touches another man's gear. Horse thieves in the old West would get strung up, a fairly mild consequence in terms of lobstering. Boats have been found adrift with nobody in them. Where the man went, nobody knows — but they said he cut the warp on his best friend's pots. One year some summer yachtsmen found a boat adrift, but this one had a man in it. Not knowing the high sophistication of a lobster war, the summer yachtsmen were

aghast to find this man insensible with the business end of a machinist's ball peen hammer sticking out of, or into, his head. After their first shock they debated if they should withdraw this or leave it for a surgeon, and as the man seemed likely to remain insensible, they prudently decided on the surgeon and towed the boat in. The man recovered, and the hammer hadn't been hurt a bit, but the day he got out of the hospital everybody watched to see who left town — this would be some indication of who first owned the hammer. A man did leave town, and he has never come back — nor will he, for the hammer is hanging in a baithouse, waiting to be claimed.

Thus it is with lobster wars, and when they start they rage furiously. The whole pattern of a region, usually so serene and industrious, sloughs off into mayhem, slaughter, and similar unpleasantries. Since a lobster war is never localized, but is watched with close interest by everybody along Maine's twenty-five-hundred-mile coastline, Dr. Gruening rightly decided this one should have all-out attention from the *News*. He dispatched his crack reportorial investigator, a real private dick character, and his best writer to Rockland, with a photographer, and before they arrived at this seaport, arrangements had been made by telephone for two charter boats to stand by and attend them. They breasted, boat to boat, down the bay for Matinicus. The trained seals were arriving to perform.

Except from a Boston paper, no such talent had ever been deployed to cover a Maine story. And they went efficiently to work. They even bolstered the sticky parts with affidavits, so witnesses wouldn't welch on them. When the story was written and the pictures made, one of the boats returned to Rockland, where an "automobile" was waiting to hurry the stuff to Portland. The reporters and the photographer stayed on Matinicus for the "follow-up."

So it needs, right now, to be explained that the lobster industry makes use of an item called a "car." It is a sort of raft, of plank-and-timber construction which floats nearly awash and has great slatted cages under it where live lobsters may be stored somewhat indefinitely. The purpose of such a car is about the same as that of a pound, a pound usually being a cove sealed off by a dam. So, the *News* reporters told of various depredations to cars, and in Portland the editors carefully corrected this to vehicles, conveyances, coaches, and automobiles. When the story came out it was one of the craziest things you ever saw.

The circulation manager, attuned to the editorial purposes, had made arrangements for extra copies of that edition to flood the coastal communities. These were snapped up, and every newsstand ordered five hundred more. The lobstermen of Maine never read anything else so funny. At Portland they started up the press and ran off some more. Dr. Gruening tried to analyze this flurry and thought it must be the editorials. There was no telephone on Matinicus in those days, so the reporters had no way of knowing what the office had done with their story until the boat came back. When they did see a copy of that *News,* they sent the boat back to Rockland at once, and in subsequent issues the *News* disregarded Dr. Gruening's style sheet, and even came right out in a headline with "car."

You will still find copies of the *News* of that date tacked up in fish houses along Maine's coast. Faded, tattered, but treasured, that paper is considered the funniest thing ever written. Which is why, long after Dr. Gruening left the State of Maine, an occasional lobsterman will get up after supper, shove his feet in his boots, and say to his wife, "Well, I think before I turn in I'll step down and check the motor vehicle."

At Last

What is now the great United States Veterans' Facility at Togus was, in the beginning, an old soldiers' home for the comrades of the Civil War. Here, in a fine, warm, congenial, comfy atmosphere a good many of the Grand Army of the Republic lingered out their days. "Facility" is perhaps the lowest word in the dictionary, suggesting chlorine-treated dinner dishes, psychiatric attention, and the clean, crisp array of clinical care. Indeed, the word "comrade" has been mislaid until it now belongs to foreigners, and consequently enemies. Nobody in his right mind would go to Togus today to have fun, but when the old soldiers lived there, everybody did. The little railroad from Randolph would bring them by the thousands for ball games, picnics, and band concerts — and to visit the comrades.

But there came, of course, a time when no such elaborate home was needed for the few old fellows who were left, and we had by that time proceeded into the era when facilities took the place of homes. In the 1920's, finally, only two old soldiers were left, and when they went out in the morning to sit in their rockers in the sun they had the place all to themselves.

They were Lemuel Attwood of Kingsbury and Saul Totman of North Yarmouth. About all they did was sit in the sun. They had told each other their war stories until there were no more to tell. But one morning Lemuel turned to Saul and interrupted the silence.

"Saul," he said, "do you remember those pills they gave us during the war to make us never-mind the girls?"

"Eyah."

"Well, by God, I believe they're beginning to take effect."

Prison Reform

When Dr. Austin Harbutt MacCormick was awarded the Bowdoin Prize in 1968 — the greatest honor that college may bestow — he was introduced from the podium as the world's leading authority on penology, prison reform, and the criminology of narcotics. He arose to receive the kudos and the cash, and then delivered his address. Those who have known Dr. Mac-Cormick, to whom he is "Spike," were not astonished at the tone of his faintly academic response. But with those who expected a dignified message about uncomfortable jails, astonishment gave way to delight as he launched into a medley of Boothbay Harbor folklore — Boothbay Harbor being (largely because of Spike) one of Maine's crystal bubbling founts of pure stuff. Originating in this lovely region, Spike had dug the clamflats mud off his boots, greased them well with Listerine, and had come to Bowdoin College to understand affairs and their causes. He somehow became interested in prison reform, and soon had himself

committed, purely for research purposes, to the Maine
State Prison at Thomaston, where he lived with and' as
the prisoners until he had the material for his thesis.
His career moved along, but his talent with the Boothbay Harbor saga has always surfaced readily to punc-
tuate his serious moments. Now, on the Bowdoin
rostrum, he punctuated liberally, and at least some few
felt he could have been honored for his folklore full as
properly as for his penology.

Dr. MacCormick's selections were of a higher quality than the run-of-the-mill Boothbay examples. He
did not, for instance, tell of the Pollard sisters, who
lived on the back road and had one set of false teeth
between them. These they used day by day, turn
about. One morning one of the sisters inserted the
teeth, because it was her day to use them, and she
sucked through them and said, "Hm-m-m, macaroons!"
This, while excellent Boothbay Harbor material,
would not be suitable at a Bowdoin College function,
and everybody was pleased that Dr. MacCormick held
to a more literary standard.

Two of his stories concern the local physician at
Boothbay Harbor, an inventive and enterprising prac-
titioner who rounded out his formal training with a
great deal of homespun talent. You might say that he
knew a lot that he never learned in school. In short, he
was the ideal man for Boothbay Harbor, where such
knowledge is not uncommon.

In one instance a family had a boy who stuttered. In his early boyhood this wasn't regarded as bad, but as he grew older the other children in school began to mock him, and his parents felt there might be some lasting effect. They brought him to the physician and asked if he could cure the boy of stuttering. He said he thought he could, but it would take a few moments to arrange the operating room, and would they take the boy away and return in about a half hour. They did, and when they came back the doctor said everything was in readiness.

He took the boy into his office and stood him before a closed closet door. Then, because of the preparations, the door suddenly flew open with a great clattering and clanging of pots and pans that had been artfully set up to do this, and there, dangling on a spring, was a human skeleton which jumped up and down as if in glee.

It cured the boy of stuttering. In fact, it frightened him so that he never spoke again and was a mute the rest of his life.

The second instance runs in somewhat the same vein. The parents brought a small boy who had somehow managed to get his head stuck in an earthenware bean pot. The physician could hear the child muttering and crying to himself inside, but a quick check showed he was getting air and there was no danger of suffocation. Yes, he said, he was sure he could remove the boy all right. Preparations were made. The examination table was made flat, with a sheet over it. An instrument tray on wheels was pushed up by the nurse, and she arranged the lighting. The doctor retired to the lavatory in the corner and washed his hands, after which the nurse helped him into his rubber surgeon's gloves. The boy was laid on the table, and carefully examined. The bean pot was surveyed from all angles. Then the doctor held up his hand for an instrument, and the nurse gave him a hammer. He hit the bean pot with the hammer, and there was the boy. The operation was entirely successful, but the shattering of the bean pot impaired the boy's hearing, and he was stone-deaf as long as he lived.

Another story related by Dr. MacCormick while accepting the Bowdoin Prize had to do with a beloved old gentleman from some place in New Jersey who used to come up to Southport to spend his summers. Southport is a town entirely on an island, just across Townshend Gut from Boothbay Harbor. This gentleman was wealthy and had a beautiful summer home. And unlike many rusticators and "summer complaints" this man had the knack of ingratiating himself and he became a great favorite of the true and year-round Southporters. It isn't everybody who can do this. Down at Calais, for example, Laban Small had lived in town ninety-two years before his death. He had been born in Canada, across the line in St.

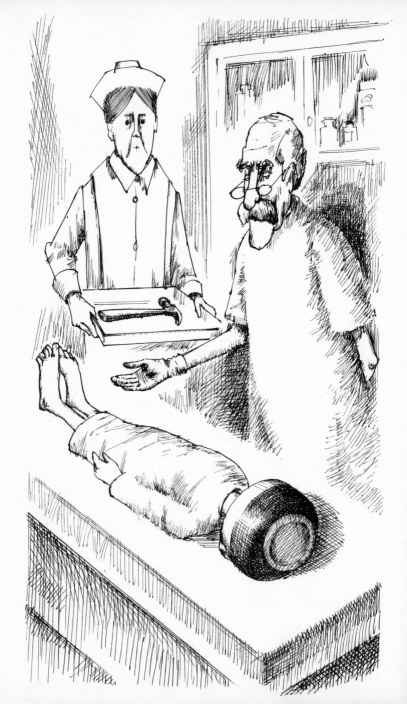

Stephen, but his parents had brought him to Calais when he was two months old. At his death, the good citizens of Calais wanted to express their affection, and they did so by causing to be inscribed on his tombstone, "He was almost one of us." This fellow from New Jersey had completely overcome such native reluctance, and was indeed one with the Southporters. Consequently the entire island was saddened to hear, one January, that he had died at his home in New Jersey. The grief was assuaged a trifle when, a few days later, word came that he had stipulated in his will that his remains were to be cremated, and his ashes scattered on Sheepscot Bay, where he had spent so many happy summer hours on his yacht. To the Southporters this seemed appropriate — it almost amounted to coming home.

But January on Sheepscot Bay, as any Southporter will state, is very different from Sheepscot Bay in July and August. So when the undertaker up at Wiscasset received the box in the mail from the crematory, he found his assignment a little difficult. Most of the boats had been taken up for the winter. But he found somebody on Juniper Point whose boat was in and who agreed to make the trip. He had some trouble finding a minister who would go out in winter to offer the essential prayer, but at last one agreed to go. It was bitter cold weather, so everybody bundled up in extra clothing. And because they would be gone all day everybody took a lunch. The day was clear, but the sharp wind that followed them out was chill, and there was something of a sea running. However, in time they arrived more or less near where the old fellow had done his yachting, and the lobsterman shut off his engine. The boat lost way and fell at once into the rote of the swells — now up and now down. Everybody had to cling to the coaming, but according to plan the exercises commenced.

The minister, on the peak of a swell, said, "Almighty God!" in excellent pulpit diction, but his voice trailed off as the boat fell into the trough. He clutched the gun'l the harder, but he kept on, and at length he boomed out his powerful Amen.

Then the undertaker reached around behind, and got the wrong box, and scattered his lunch upon the waves.

Other Ashes

Crematory lore, additional to Dr. MacCormick's fine example, may be cited before the subject is changed:

Stanley Purcelle was a farmer at Point Agreeable. He had bought the old Noble place from Augustus M. Noble, last of the Noble family. Augustus Noble had, as a young man, gone to New York and become both successful and wealthy. He had no interest in the old homestead back in Maine, so had sold it to Stanley Purcelle at a very fair price — but with the condition that he might come up if the mood struck him and do some vacationing. He did come a few times, but in late years had not. But when he died he requested that his ashes be scattered on the old family acres at Point Agreeable. Thus, one morning in the mail, Stanley Purcelle received the ashes, with a request that they be strewn.

It happened to be in the springtime of the year, and Mr. Purcelle was busy preparing his land for the season's crops. Being eager to get his work done, but being equally eager to carry out the last wish of Mr. Noble, he combined both tasks with equal success. He put Mr. Noble's ashes on top of the load in his manure spreader, and then he spread the load.

Another excellent Maine story in this vein concerns a family at Tenants Harbor. A lobsterman, Mr. Hartford Cook, would occasionally indulge a certain summer resident and permit him to ride out in the boat while Harty hauled his pots. The man was something of a nuisance to Harty, frequently standing around in the way, but Harty is a pleasant fellow and he put up with it because he knew it meant so much to the guest. And it did mean much to him. Besides the status that came from being privileged to fish with a lobsterman of Harty's prominence, there was the adventure of the sea and beauty of wind, sky, and tide. This fellow often said that the happiest hours of his life were spent with Harty Cook on his boat. Years rolled by, and it had been a long time since Harty had seen the man.

And it happened that one winter, when fishing is at ebb, Harty went to remodeling his home. He undertook a major change. He took out partitions, put on additions, and spent a great deal of time and money. Among other things, he contrived for his wife Marge a large and beautiful living room — something the home had not enjoyed and about which she frequently murmured. Everything was the best. Wall-to-wall carpets, smooth paneling, correct lighting — everything. The room was to be, easily, the finest of its kind in Tenants Harbor, and when it was finished it was a room that everybody admired and oh'd about the instant he stepped into it. Marge was proud as could be, and after all those years of lacking a real living room she set about making the most of her joy.

At precisely this moment one of the little packages came in the mail for Harty, and he was saddened to hear that his onetime fishing companion had died in New York. The ashes were being forwarded, said a letter from the executor of the estate, according to decedent's last wish — that his good friend and old companion would scatter them over the wild turbulence of Skintight Shoals, where he and Harty had often gone. Harty was touched.

Unfortunately, in the long years of meantime, oceanographers had reported that the mean temperature of the Gulf of Maine had changed, and that accordingly there had been a change in the habits of the Maine lobster. Harty, without any help from the oceanographers, had noticed this himself, and he had greatly changed his fishing habits. He gave up his old grounds and found new ones where the lobsters had gone, presumably because of the changing temperatures. In short, he hadn't been anywhere near Skintight Shoals in a good many seasons, and he had no intentions, and no reason, to go over that way in the near future.

So it happened that the poor man's ashes were set up on the mantel in Marge's new living room, to await the day when some oddity of chance would take Harty over to Skintight Shoals, and he hasn't done so yet.

Marge's new living room thus was dubbed "The Mortuary" and this somewhat dimmed her initial pleasure at its completion. Folklore being what it is, the room will probably remain The Mortuary forever — or at least until Harty Cook finds some reason to go over to Skintight Shoals.

Water Witching

The word dowsing was little used throughout Maine until the novelist Kenneth Roberts turned his attention to the subject and introduced Henry Gross to literature. Roberts treated the subject so fully that much of the mysticism evaporates in boredom, but he did popularize the term dowsing — which had always pretty much been called witching. Henry Gross was a county agent for what used to be called the Farm Bureau and is now the Extension Service. As many another could, he was able to walk about with a hazel switch, or some other divining rod, and locate underground water. He perfected this until he became a dowser, or water witch, who could locate veins and domes without even stepping on the land — he could do it over a map or sketch. Kenneth Roberts embraced this faith, and at a time he should have been devoting his fine talent to significant historical novels, he wrote, instead, a trilogy that extolled and defended Henry Gross, and vilified all nonbelievers. (*Henry Gross and his Dowsing Rod; The Seventh Sense; Water Unlimited* — Doubleday.)

Hardly anybody in Maine ever doubted, folklore or

fact, that water may be dowsed. Almost everybody has seen a dowser locate water by walking about until his stick dips down, and it's much like Amos Grayson of North Whitefield, who was asked if he believed in infant baptism. Amos said, "Hell, yes — I've seen it done!" That settles that.

So Maine had, and still has, a great many water witches (the term is bisexual) who could find water just as well as Henry Gross ever did, and were somewhat put out at Author Roberts. Some of them deplored the exploitation of so mystical a gift. It was like divulging the secret of a Master Mason. In a sense, there was a feeling that Henry Gross had deserted the ranks and had taken his thirty pieces of silver to join the literary set. There was an amateur status, and while it was all right for a water witch to take a five-dollar bill for finding well water, it was another thing to have a Boswell, an incorporation, a bank account, and fame. While Henry Gross was finding water all right, and doing fine, whenever he stepped out to spend a little money, or go to the bank, he would find other water witches sneering at him.

Water witching is not unlike taking a listener survey for television and radio. These surveys ascertain only who is listening and what they are listening to. The nonlistener, and the program not worth attending, are never in the statistics. There is, similarly, no testimony about the times that water witching didn't work. (I, myself, can walk about with a forked stick, and it will dip down beautifully upon occasion. I am thus a water witch, I suppose, and anybody who sees my stick dip down will admit that I have the seventh sense. But nobody has ever dug a hole to see if I am right. Thus it is.) The following bit of water-witching folklore would have sent Kenneth Roberts into delightful rebuttal, had he known about it and had he deemed it a slight on his Henry Gross, but it is typical of many dowsing stories around about the State of Maine, and probably deserves neither pro nor con.

Walter Maybury needed a well. Many a Maine farm had gone along for generations with water supplies provided in colonial days, but times changed. A well which had adequately watered the farm stock, and by the bucketful had supplied the household needs, couldn't keep up with modern plumbing after an electric pump was installed. Walter was in this fix. His old well had seemed fine, and it was excellent water, but lately he had refurbished his home. The upstairs bathroom, the downstairs half bathroom, the laundry, the dishwasher — these simply used more water than the farm had previously required. Now Walter had to find a new supply, and he consulted a well driller. The well driller came and looked the situation over. And he said something which all honest well drillers should say here in Maine, where dowsing is common. It went like this: "Now, if you leave it to me, I'd drill right here;

but if you believe in witching and want to do it some place else, it's all one with me and I'll go down wherever you say."

At this time Mr. Maybury was open-minded. He neither believed nor disbelieved in dowsing. He just hadn't thought about it. That is to say, he was aware that dowsing existed, but it didn't occur to him to turn to it even when he was considering a well. So he smiled and was a moment amused at the obvious disclaimer of the well driller, and then he decided that since drilling a well is a sizable expense he might as well cover all angles. So he went over on the back road and called on Ronald Sanborn, who was a reputable water witch, and Ronnie came over with his stick the next day and dowsed.

This is truly something to see if you never have. The two ends of a limber crotch from a tree or bush are held in the hands, leaving the singular end free to dip down when the magic moment comes. What causes it to dip is what all the fighting is about, and for some people who lack the gift it never will dip. With Ronnie it dipped finally, and he made several passes to confirm his spot. "Right here!" he said, and he stuck down a little stick. "Fourteen feet down, you'll get all the water you want."

The amusement with which Mr. Maybury first approached the suggestion of a dowser had by now nurtured a little curiosity, and being a thoughtful man he decided on some insurance. He drove over to the next town to see a Mrs. Ruth Goodwell, who was also a reputable dowser, and without telling her that Ronnie Sanborn had already dowsed the field he inquired if she would favor him. Before she came, Mr. Maybury removed Ronnie's little stick, but triangulated the spot so he could find it exactly again. When Mrs. Goodwell came she did about as Ronnie had done, and coursed back and forth as in a trance, waiting for the stick to tell her something. When she got a response, it was where Ronnie had got his, and after several passes she said, "Right here! Down about fifteen feet, I'd say." When she set her little stick in the ground Mr. Maybury knew it was close, but after she left he triangulated the spot and her stick was precisely where Ron's had been.

Mr. Maybury was not a little caught up with the whole thing, and it was hard for him to believe that these two dowsers could have found the same spot without collusion. He accordingly drove some thirty miles in another direction and inquired if any dowsers lived about, and he found a man who guaranteed to find him water or there would be no charge. The man came, and he was such a total stranger that he kept calling Mr. Maybury "Mr. Bradbury," and after he paddled back and forth a half hour or so he said, "Right here! Can't say how far down for sure, but it's a good vein, and not over twenty feet." Mr. Maybury first noticed and afterwards proved that the dowser had set down his little stick exactly where Ronald Sanborn and Mrs. Goodwell had put theirs. Dowsing never had better proof.

"I think I'll have you drill right here," said Mr. Maybury to the well driller, and he indicated the spot on which the three dowsers had independently agreed. "Anywhere you say," said the well driller, and he set up and went down seven hundred and eighty feet without finding a drop of water.

They abandoned that hole, and the well driller said, "I told you first off, if it'd been me, I'd-a set up over there next the house. Myself, I don't believe in witching, but I have to play along with it."

So the well driller set up over by the house, where he had first indicated, and he went down eight hundred and thirty feet and he didn't find any water there, either.

All this activity had been an enormous expense to Mr. Maybury, so he called the thing off. All that next winter he lifted water from his old well with a pail, and it seemed a shame to have toilets, bath, laundry and sink that they couldn't use. The following summer he was wandering around thinking things over, and he took a fresh look at the lay of his land, and he noticed it came down this way from one side, and so-fashion on the other, and he half convinced himself that if he was a vein of water flowing along he'd almost do it about so . . .

The more he thought about it, the more reasonable it seemed, so he got a post-hole auger, and several lengths of pipe so he could extend the handle, and he began screwing the thing into the ground to see what he might see. At ten feet down he uncovered a boiling spring that gushed up through his auger hole and started a small brook down across the field. So he got his water, and that's about the size of it with dowsers and well drillers, and Mr. Maybury says that water witching certainly works because he's seen it done.

Cause and Effect

Captain Clarence Meservey of Brooklin tells of a neighbor of his who began to detect a fault in his well water. He immediately sent to the State Department of Health and Welfare in Augusta for one of the glass bottles. This department, free of charge, will analyze well water, and if something is believed wrong, make suggestions as to a correction. The bottle came promptly, so the Brooklin farmer filled it and mailed it back, and the statehouse laboratory ran a test.

The results were so pronounced that they didn't wait to get a letter off — they called the farmer right up, and they said not to touch that water. It was in bad shape. They said it was so bad they were sending an inspector down the next day, and not to use the water until he got there.

The inspector came, and after a quick look around he surmised that the family cesspool was in such a location that seepage was possible, and he said, "I think you'd better stop using that cesspool, and relo-cate another off in that direction."

So they stopped using the cesspool, and the well
up.

g
e-
for
beds
dry
use a

flywheel,
flywheel
water in
a no'theast
all similar
n was never
was even more

n't Take Much

an to become practical for small
on Custom House Wharf in
successful model that had
hing better came along.
it was the Smith &
'd see that the era of
uld have a motor,
g but a smooth
n't that good,

yet, but you could walk home from a highway break-
down. The safest innovation was to put an engine in a
sloop, and if the old putt-putt conked out you could up-
sail and get back. So quite a few years passed before
machines could be trusted, and in that period the
Smith & Langmaid took its rightful place in the folklore of the Maine coast.

It was a fairly simple machine. The single cylinder
was housed in an upright block, and the head was six
or eight inches in diameter, with a long stroke. The
piston rod attached to a crank on the shaft. The spark
plug on top was set off by a "make and break" contact
which, in turn, was activated by the action of the
cylinder. That's about all there was to it, but since it
was simple and direct it had to be lined up right along
the keel, and this wasn't so good. Well, being a one
lunger, the motor depended on a heavy flywheel
momentum, and because of the low-slung engine
the flywheel would turn in the bilgewater. A
lobsterboat is a very good thing to have if you
Smith & Langmaid, but . . .

Nobody had thought yet about an inclosed
so usually, as a fisherman doddled out, his
would be churning up the bilge and heavin
the air so he might as well have been in
rain. On the Smith & Langmaid, as on
engines of the time, the spark igniti
steady, and for this reason the flywheel

important — it kept the engine going until it could make up its mind to fire again. On cordwood saw rigs for the farms, a one-cylinder engine often didn't fire for three or four minutes, but thanks to the flywheel the men would keep on sawing wood. The same principle of inertia would keep a boat going, too, but it was far more disconcerting at sea to have an engine that sounded as if it were always about to stop. The Smith & Langmaid imparted to lobstering a peculiarity — the engine would putt-putt-skip-skip-skip-putt, and give to fishermen of the day a certain haunted cast of perpetual wonderment, and they always seemed to be listening for something nobody else could hear. And unless they pumped their bilge they would strike out on a bright, sunny day wearing their weather gear.

There was no starter on a Smith & Langmaid, and it took a little know-how to start one — something like doing brain surgery. The huge flywheel had a kind of handle on a spring that pulled out and made a crank, receding by itself when not needed. The trick was to bring the flywheel up so compression was gained in the cylinder head, previous to which there might be some priming with raw gasoline, and then when the feet were braced right, and you had a lull in the tide swell, a good stiff yank against the compression (if the cussid sparker went off) might start things going. If it did, there would be a pop, and the flywheel would jerk out of your hand, the little handle thing would recede, and

if God was sitting right on your shoulder the boat would take off. There was no clutch, but a man could reverse his boat by making the Smith & Langmaid run backwards — which it would do, throwing water from the other side. Usually, on a cold morning when all the fishermen were trying at once to start their boats, the combined profanity made the air quite comfortable, and sometimes would singe the paint on buildings along the waterfront.

But all the same, the Smith & Langmaid has its place in longshore lore, and for a good many years the engine patiently conditioned fishermen to the motor age. Strangely enough, the best folk story about the Smith & Langmaid is not of saltwater origin at all, but comes from Rangeley Lake, where in those early days the management of the Lake House decided to acquire a motorboat for the pleasure of the guests. It arrived one June, equipped with a Smith & Langmaid engine, and it was put overboard with fitting ceremonies. She was twenty-six feet long, intended to sail parties around the lake to inspect the natural beauties.

The Rangeley Lakes Hotel was called the Lake House by Rangeley people, and being on the style of the Poland Spring and Crawford Notch resorts was plush and large. It maintained an excellent dining room, and spared nothing to give every courtesy and service to its guests. Like most of its kind, it became a white elephant when the eras shifted, and ceased. But its location was superb, and it gave on the great expanse of one of the world's most beautiful lakes. Before it were the beaches, and also wharves and piers for the canoes and rowboats. And along the whole stretch of the lake front, running right around the entire point of land, was a long, wide boardwalk much admired by the guests, who pounded away at it for their constitutionals between meals. The new power-boat was tied to a float right by this boardwalk, which made a fine gallery for inspections.

And everybody came to see the boat. The hotel guests signed up for rides. Townspeople walked over to look. And particularly the guides, for they were greatly excited at the idea of motors — they paddled and rowed all day, and this seemed like a great rising sun on the horizon of their future. There was, however, one guide who didn't come and look the new boat over.

He was Ralph Philbrick. Ralph had left just before the boat arrived to guide some canoeists up the Magalloway River to Parmachenee Lake, and he didn't get back to town until the initial excitement over the boat had subsided. When he did come over to look at her, there was nobody around except the young Rangeley man who had been hired to operate her and who was now being called "Cap'n" by his friends. Ralph came down and stood on the boardwalk where he could see the boat, and he said, "Hello, Jack!"

Jack looked up and invited Ralph aboard, beginning

at once to explain the marvels of this fine new motor. He pointed out the priming cup, the handle on the flywheel, and described the principle. Ralph was truly impressed. And then Jack said, "Want to go for a ride?"

The lines were cast off, and while Ralph watched, young Jack primed the cup, brought the flywheel up on compression, and finally spun the thing so it putted. Then it putted again, and again, and since there was no clutch the boat started moving and Ralph was more than impressed — he was thrilled. Putt-putt, it went, and then it would skip-putt and then it would putt-skip, and the flywheel was doing fine. As they moved out, Ralph looked behind him as he sat on the seat, and he noticed that a summer guest at the hotel had come down to the boardwalk and was starting his constitutional in the same direction the boat was taking — scarce ten feet away. Then the motor went skip-putt-skip, and then it went putt-skip-putt, and things seemed to be going just splendidly, and Jack looked up and said. "There! She's wide open now!"

Indeed she was. Ralph could see that. The boat smoothly moved along — a great sight for a man who lives with oars. It was almost too much to credit. Then Ralph looked toward the shore, and he saw that the summer guest walking on the boardwalk was keeping right up with them. He was strolling along, and the motor was going putt-skip, and it was nip and tuck.

Shortly, however, Ralph noticed that the guest was gaining a little, and was now walking on ahead of the boat.

Then Jack observed that Ralph was making this comparison to himself, and it tarnished a little bit the pride the young man had in his boat. In turn, Ralph saw that Jack had noticed and was hurt a little. But Ralph looked again, and now the guest was a good ways ahead, and the boat was "wide open."

Ralph had to say something. He said, "And he ain't much of a walker, either!"

It may not be the best State of Maine remark about the Smith & Langmaid marine engine, but it has the merit of being printable.

Toplofty's Bereavement

Toplofty Jim Manfred was sitting in his alleged living room one fine sabbath afternoon, meditating as was his wont, when he was disturbed by a thump upon his portal, and he opened it to find a dark-suited gentleman of dignified appearance looking a bit bewildered, and Jim said, "Yes?"

"I beg your pardon," said the gentleman, "but I

mistrust I am at the wrong door. I was seeking the
Gibson sisters."

"You are one mile and three doors off," said Toplofty Jim, at which the gentleman, by way of explanation, said, "I am the Reverend Homer F. Thorndale,
new pastor at the Methodist Church."

"I think I could have guessed it," said Toplofty Jim
pleasantly. "But now that you're here, why don't you
come in?"

The minister hesitated, but only briefly, and he
stepped inside where Toplofty Jim pulled a hound out
of a Morris chair and motioned affably for the parson
to sit, while the hound looked over his shoulder with a
certain disdain for the clergy.

"I have had no ecclesiastical visitations in recent
times," said Toplofty Jim, "and I scarce know the
amenities. I happen to be refreshing myself, but I
don't know if I should offer you the same — it's grape
juice and vodka."

"Thank you," said Mr. Thorndale, "but it would not
be seemly. Please, however, continue as you were,
although I might accompany you with a sip of plain
grape juice."

"I am not," said Toplofty Jim as he poured out a
glass, "much of a church man, although I am kind,
pleasant, and harmless, but I have some reputation as
a genial host — are you sure a touch of vodka wouldn't
help make you ready for the Gibson sisters?"

"Ha-ha," said Mr. Thorndale, who had found himself becoming greatly interested in this huge man, "dear me, no."

"I'm glad you mistook yourself to my door," said Toplofty Jim. "Oftentimes somebody drops in on Sundays to speed the interim before the prandial hour, but today I was alone and found the clock dragging. How long you been in town?"

Then there followed some small talk, and at one point Mr. Thorndale said, "Frankly, I'm somewhat amazed. You converse rather well, and I should not expect this from the location, the surroundings, and your appearance. I suspect you have had formal education."

"Yes," said Toplofty Jim. "I have my baccalaureate and my master's, but I don't work at it. I prefer the quiet life, sort of halfway between the Wild Man of Borneo and Henry David Thoreau. I am not a recluse, but I find there are times when solitude is more fun than socializing."

"Very interesting," said Mr. Thorndale. "I find your company delightful. You know, being a minister has the one great drawback that you must live your business at all times. Everybody else can go home from his work, or come in from the fields, but there is an intellectual loneliness to being a pastor. This is why I find your company refreshing. I'm delighted that I missed the Gibson sisters today. I believe I can confide in you that visiting the Gibson sisters hardly gives one a view of the great flow of mankind."

"Hardly," said Toplofty Jim. "Well, you feel free to indulge this great yearning for truth and light, and you just drop in whenever the mood strikes you. As long as you don't drink my vodka and don't try to bring me to my pagan knees, you're as welcome as the flowers that bloom in the spring."

"This pleases me. I am not rebellious. It's more, as you say, a yearning. I hope I may feel welcome when occasion offers."

So they discoursed pleasantly, and at one time Mr. Thorndale said, "Do you keep any livestock, Mr. Manfred?"

Toplofty Jim said, "Yes — I have two milking cows, a heifer, a bull, a pair of steers, a horse, two sheep, and a — well, that is to say, I have a — well, pardon me, Reverend, but I have, I mean, a donkey, let's say."

"I can readily see," said Mr. Thorndale, "why you would want to keep a donkey, but whatever do you do with the other beasts?"

"Touché!" said Toplofty Jim. "It is my turn to cry ha-ha. You are quite right. But it is my indulgence. All my life, ever since I was a small boy, I have had a great desire to own a jack — that is, a donkey, and it never came to pass. I had a chance to pick one up a while back, and I just couldn't forbear. He's a cute

little jack — er, that is, I mean donkey — and I find
him good company, and he fulfills my boyish whim."

There was more of this for a time, and then Mr.
Thorndale said, "Mr. Manfred, it amuses me to detect
in your euphemistical use of the word 'donkey' a certain nicety that may be criticized. I am looking
through the window, and I can see your jackass on his
tether, and several times you have started to call him
one thing, but have hesitated and called him another.
Are you favoring the cloth?"

"Yes, I am," said Toplofty Jim. "I just can't help it.
It's a mess of old-fashioned Calvinistic froth, but I
just can't bring myself to it. Here in Maine, where the
long vowels sometimes flatten in the *patois*, there is a
startling similarity betwixt the name of a lowly beast
of burden and the posterior anatomy of the human-
kind."

"True," said Mr. Thorndale. "But there seems to be
little *veritas* in your vodka. This is a silly absurdity.
Your values are muddled. The word that you are
avoiding is a perfectly good word, and I accuse you of
a snide nicety."

"I suspect so," said Toplofty Jim.

"It's true. You profess indifference to church, pro-
claim meditation is your pleasure, yet you flinch at
saying the simple word *ass* in my ministerial presence.
On the other hand, I — who avoid the uncouth and
indelicate as a prerequisite of my profession — can

speak the word *ass* with no qualms and no off-color connotations."

"You're partly right," said Toplofty Jim. "But this isn't something that happens just because you're here. I live with it. I know there's nothing wrong with the word *ass,* but here in Maine it *sounds* wrong. No amount of rationalizing removes the jolt everybody gets when I say that I rode up through the pasture on my ass."

"No need of a jolt at all," said Mr. Thorndale. "Christ rode from Dan to Beersheba on his ass, and it has been in sacred literature for two thousand years."

"Eyah," said Toplofty Jim. "But he didn't do it in the State of Maine. Some things you just have to talk around. You hear people say they are going to go and call on the Smiths, or the Johnsons. But nobody ever says he's going to visit the Hoars. He always makes it very clear that it's the Joseph Hoar family, or something like that. Joe's a good fellow, although childish in his politics, but he just happens to have a name that always sounds wrong. And to me, and to others, the word *ass* always calls for a flip-flop."

"This is ridiculous," said Mr. Thorndale.

"No it is not," said Toplofty Jim. "I always get a mental shock when somebody comes up and says, 'How's your ass?' "

"Utterly ridiculous," said Mr. Thorndale. "Why, the Scriptures are literally riddled with the word *ass*. It is a good pulpit word. Abraham said to abide with the ass; Issachar was likened to a strong ass; Balaam smote his ass three times when it turned and spoke to him; it's even in the Commandments — thou shalt not covet thy neighbor's ass. All through the Bible. In terms of Holy Writ, *ass* is a perfectly good word."

"I know you're right," said Toplofty Jim, "but I still hesitate to tell people my ass has a rash and brays all night."

Anyway, soon after that Toplofty Jim's ass, or donkey, died. And not knowing of this bereavement, the Reverend Mr. Homer F. Thorndale, having a mood to visit Toplofty Jim, came to the farm and found Toplofty Jim out behind the barn digging a grave. They exchanged greetings, and then the Reverend Homer F. Thorndale said, "What are you doing, Mr. Manfred, digging a posthole?"

Toplofty Jim replied, "In terms of Holy Writ, Reverend — the answer is no."

Alexander G. Clapper

For some years there was a quick way to get attention from the telephone company in Maine, but time has faded the sheen and you don't hear it so much now. It

came out of a crusade by the old Lisbon *Enterprise,*
which was caused by the great indifference of the
telephone company about a thing they like to call
service. We weren't getting any. The statistics were
forceful. The community had less than five thousand
inhabitants, but was supporting over fifteen hundred
telephones — a pretty good average for anywhere. And
although many a town which was putting far less
money into the company coffers was getting new
equipment and new exchanges, we were still cranking
away at our old magneto system, and if we could raise
Central the custom was to shout, "Beano!"

The crusade didn't begin in the newspaper. At home
we had a "four-party line," and while it began honestly
enough as a four-party line the thing was now gonging
day and night with seventeen rings. Eighteen, really,
because one ring was the signal to Central. With this
number of subscribers on a "four-party" line the
mechanics of the equipment failed. When we cranked
our instrument with the idea of giving a number to
Central, the electric impulse thus generated wasn't
strong enough to ring the bells in sixteen other homes
and still knock down the flap on the central switch-
board. We were all paying, of course, the long price for
a four-party line, just as if we had one, and Central
would sit there on her stool without knowing if we
were alive or dead.

I got in touch with the regional manager and asked a

few questions, and he said he would look into it. After a time, without hearing from him, I called him back and was told that he had stepped out. It was curious — if I had somebody else call him, he would be right there at his desk, but if I called, he had just stepped out. I drove up to the city and walked in on him before he saw me coming, and he babbled quite some time about service, and recited sections of the company manual that tells how to meet the public. He insisted I was on a four-party line, but under pressure he explained that the former four-party lines were now all eight-party lines. I asked him about the other nine rings, and he denied there was any such thing. He said, "From your smile, I gather you don't believe me." I said no, that I didn't believe a word he said, and that he was a cockeyed liar, and that's when the *Enterprise* started its crusade.

Bringing the great New England Telephone & Telegraph Company to heel is an ambitious undertaking for an obscure country weekly with a large mortgage, so we planned the thing carefully. We sat with our feet up, off and on, for about two weeks, chewing things over, and before we sprung the thing we had our program ready for three months' issues. We thought we knew at just what point the Field Representative would come in to assure us Lisbon was "on the list." Then we would ask to see the list. There wasn't any list, and they knew it and we knew it, but "the list" was bandied about to placate the growing public complaint. And it worked out just as we surmised.

The crusade was a complete hoax in which the entire town joined. It began with a small paragraph buried in the personal column that a group of men interested in forming a telephone company had met at the home of Mr. Elliot K. Hale. Mrs. Hale, it said, had served a dainty collation.

This was followed the next week by another item saying that the men had decided to proceed, and had retained the services of a Mr. Alexander G. Clapper, who would handle all details, including the financing. The next week Mr. Clapper announced that a bond issue, convertible to stock, was being subscribed, and money appeared to be easy. Then we let the thing ride for two weeks. We never came right out and said so, but the idea was that while the telephone company had their Bell, we had the clapper. And we knew that the telephone company subscribed to a clipping agency, so that even our back-page items would find their way to the top.

At this point we found that we had a friend in a high place. This friend worked in the Portland office of the company, and was getting much amusement out of the interoffice memos that flew around every time our paper came out. In a social context this friend kept us informed; we never violated any confidence and we never made use of what we learned this way, but it was great fun to be privy to the furor we were stirring up. I suppose this friend did aid us in making an occasional shrewd guess.

There was another friend who helped. In those days Everett M. Smith was assistant city editor of the *Christian Science Monitor,* and he was a photographer. We turned to him, and all the illustrations for our crusade were made in the publishing house darkrooms by Everett. He made up a whole sequence, for the duration. He came up with a wonderful portrait of Alexander G. Clapper, who turned out to be Everett M. Smith. So, with a photograph, we came out with a story of a mass meeting in Lisbon, where telephone bonds sold like hot cakes and various respected citizens extolled the Clapper project. There never was such a meeting, but we ran a list of the people present. Phil Allen, who neglected to tell his wife that he was in on the hoax, said she was reading the paper that week and she said, "So that's where you were!" At that meeting Professor Clapper (we also called him *Dr*. Clapper by times) outlined his plans. He said his invention would eventually take the place of conventional telephones and probably would put the New England out of business in a year or so. Our friend in the Portland office said the excitement ran high.

Next, we revealed what the Clapper invention was. He took two cans and tied them together with string. Any boy knows that the bottom of a tin can will vibrate and perform like a diaphragm, and you can hear the vibrations in another tin can at a distance if you keep the string tight. This invention was hailed appropriately, and in an editorial we commented that this was infinitely better than anything now in use in town. So the next week we started a string-saving campaign, with captains on every street and a prize for the biggest ball of twine turned in before Tuesday. Dr. Clapper needed all the string he could get. There was what purported to be a "Public Notice," saying the town officials would hold a hearing on easements. We ran a photograph of Dr. Clapper looping some string through a lilac bush. Then we went to the canning factory of Burnham & Morrill and borrowed their stockpile long enough to get a picture of a mountain of cans. We showed the six-party can and the ten-party can.

Now came another photograph from Everett Smith. He put a very pretty girl in a bathing suit on a stool, and in one hand she held a Spanish-English dictionary, the other hand had a tin can to her ear. On the other portion of the picture was good old Dr. Clapper, talking to her over a length of string. A broken line down the center indicated that the photograph was made up from two separate negatives. We printed it, and announced that Dr. Clapper had inaugurated toll service to South America. We couldn't help it, and the caption was, "Come here, Dr. Clapper, I want you."

Ridiculing the telephone company now completely absorbed us. Apart from the young man who had come in as we foresaw and insisted we were on the "list," we had had no official approach, but now we got one. The regional manager who had so often been out paid us a visit. He came in looking fairly silly, hat in hand, and he hemmed and hawed, protesting his sunny disposition and friendly nature, and after a bit he said he wondered if he could speak to Mr. Clapper. It is, and was, incredible that he was taken in by this nonsense, but if you pause to analyze a telephone man's mind, you realize that with pressure on him from upstairs he was in trouble. All the memos and all the telephone calls came finally to his desk, and after enough of that, he'd believe anything. But I was so unready to credit his gullibility that I almost gave the thing away to his face. Then I knew that what I needed most — being alone in the office — was a witness. So I said, "Hm-m, let me see . . ." and I cranked the telephone. I was pleased that the operator didn't respond right away and I had to crank three times. When she came on, I said, "Would you ring me Judge Jack?"

I asked Judge Jack if Mr. Clapper might be in his office. Judge Jack had followed our telephone campaign closely and had offered several fine suggestions, so he laughed like hell. I said, "I have a man in the office here who wants to meet him." Then I made the same call to Arthur Lawrence in the drugstore. Neither

Jack nor Lawrence were ever slow on the draw, so presently they came loping into the *Enterprise* office to see who wanted to meet Clapper, and the regional manager was in the record.

It wasn't long after that the thing came to a head. We still had a lot more Clapper stuff ready to print, but one day two men from the telephone company called on us, and we didn't have to use it. I was sorriest when I tossed in the junk box an engraving of Dr. Clapper making a trans-Atlantic cable from brown shoestrings. It was the best of the Smith pictures, showing the great intellect of the man — Everett Smith, that is, not Dr. Clapper. But out it went, and the crusade was over. The two men came in an expensive company car and brought me an advance news story prepared just for us. No other paper got it. It said work would start at once on a complete, new, dial system for Lisbon. A contract to construct a new central office had just been signed with Merle Brown, local builder. They also gave us a special paid advertisement, just for us, that had been prepared by their agency, Doremus & Co., the outfit that God went with when He was voted out of Batten, Barton, Durstine & Osborn. Soon after that we had as good telephone service as anybody.

Some years later, a telephone executive who mellowed a little during some social discourse admitted that Professor Clapper had gained Lisbon its new system at least a full seven years before the company had any intentions of making a move. Ordinary complaints, he said, the company knows how to handle — but the continued ridicule was too much for them. "You almost drove our regional manager crazy — you know that, don't you?" he asked. "We had to move him to a quieter office, and after a while he was all right again. He thought Clapper was after his job." It just now occurs to me that I never did see that regional manager again.

And Mr. Clapper, having accomplished his purpose, also departed. We never saw him again. But for a long time after that, and even once in a while yet, if somebody gets mad at the telephone company in these parts he will ring up the regional manager and commence negotiations by saying, "Hello, this is Alexander G. Clapper speaking . . ."

The Proper Time

Curiously, there appears little folklore in Maine about the long era of the Volstead bootlegger. An occasional anecdote, but not the great volume to be expected. Perhaps this is because national prohibition came on the tag end of Maine's own extended drought, and nothing much that happened was too different from what was going on anyway. Maine citizens had early adopted the political philosophy of "vote dry and drink wet," and this was so ingrained in the mores that another dry law or two made no nevermind. Even today certain opponents of spirits will appear at statehouse hearings to state their public opinions with private hangovers. The evils of John Barleycorn have had every legislative restraint in Maine, as befits a hard-drinking people.

In the great days of sail, hardly a family in Maine was without its deepwater skipper and his own vessel, and intoxicants, along with lumber, slaves, tea, guano, and piracy, were a staple item. This was not always so stated in the polite records, and one must read between the lines. Take the frustrating voyage of Captain Theodore Wells, of Wells, who sailed his schooner *Friendship* to the West Indies with a cargo of Maine timber. His owners told him not to dispose of it unless he could get a hundred gallons of molasses for each thousand feet of lumber. He found the market depressed, and still asking his price he touched at St. Vincents, Grenada, Trinidad, Port Royal on Martinico, Guadaloupe, Nevis, St. Thomas, Porto Rico, St. Domingo, Aux Cayes, Jérémie, Mariguana, Port-au-Prince, and St. Marks. None of these stops would give him what he asked. Thus the student of maritime history has a pretty picture of a schooner running about, and understands how trading was done in those days, but there is no emphasis on his purpose — to bring back molasses for the rum mills. Having access to the vintages and beverages of the world, and with a great percentage of her people afloat, Maine was lawfully dry as a bone, but her people knew a good brandy when it was poured.

I have reported elsewhere the story of the deacon at Richmond who used to cruise down to Portsmouth, New Hampshire, every June and fetch home a cask of rum, which he broached on a sawhorse under the trees in his dooryard. When haying started, the deacon's haymakers were free to approach it. Nobody else in the whole area could hire haymakers — they were all over working for the deacon.

Other farmers persuaded the minister to speak to the deacon about this unfair practice, and among other things, he said it was unbecoming a deacon of the church to use intoxicating beverages to his advantage. "I suggest you take some of your good springwater," he said, "and mix it with oatmeal, molasses, and ginger, and it will make you a most refreshing drink that will be a good deal better for you than rum."

The deacon said he didn't want anything better than rum.

Cruising down to Portsmouth was by no means uncommon. A market in that city maintained a wharf at the waterfront, and every day the wagon would come down and pick up the jugs brought in by boats from Maine. Each jug would have a name tagged to it, with instructions for what was to be inserted. As the wagon returned the jugs, the boats would head down harbor back to their Maine ports. A sloop from Muscongus Bay would have jugs aboard for most of the teetotaler households from Pemaquid to Port Clyde. And for highlander palates, there was the proximity of Canada. Woodsmen had well-trod trails over the boundary and used to tote the stuff back in packsacks. Since bottled liquors are weighty, a good man would always take two packsacks — the "walk and hide" method. He'd carry one basket two or three miles and hide it. Then he'd go back and get his second basket, and advance it two or three miles beyond the first one. Advancing each in turn, thus, he would get home with a double load — and don't worry, woodsmen tested it out and knew that this method was faster and easier than making two separate trips.

And if a State of Mainer had no sloop, no pack basket, and no friends going to New Hampshire and Canada, there was always the thoughtful loophole of the state's dry law — the legality of booze for "mechanical and medicinal purposes." Anybody who couldn't qualify as a mechanic could always take sick. It was a rare Maine home, indeed, which didn't have a bottle of whiskey laid by, ready for any illness. Occasionally an antique shop will offer an interesting item

— the "captain's companion" of an old sailing vessel. This is a wooden chest of great beauty and cunning, fitted with decanters and glasses. The customary three bottles would offer gin, rum, and whiskey and the glasses were sufficient to accommodate any guests the skipper might have in his cabin — particularly customs officers. The chests were perhaps not remarkable by themselves; it was remarkable that every vessel sailing from abstemious Maine had one.

So when the United States went dry all over, it was nothing new to Maine. About the only difference was the great increase in smuggling as the gangsters made use of Maine's long and irregular coastline. Here was a stretch of twenty-five hundred miles — longer than all the rest of our Atlantic shore from Portsmouth to Key West — that defied the Coast Guard and revenue agents. Nobody could patrol that. The occasional seizure of a load or two of liquor was but a drop in the bucket. The landing and transportation of liquor destined for speakeasies in Boston, Providence, New York, and Philadelphia were arranged and carried out by big shots in those places, and not too many Maine people came to know much about that. Fishermen who brought the stuff in from the "mother ship" outside were told only two things — where to get it and where to leave it.

There was some risk, and once in a while somebody got caught, but mostly rumrunning was uneventful.

After picking up his load outside, a lobsterman who was helping the smugglers would start at full throttle for the shore. If the Coast Guard gave chase he had all the advantages. Having timed his run with the tide, he would pass over some reef just at the last possible moment to do so safely. His keel would bruise the rockweed, and inches below would be jagged rocks that could tear his planks apart. Minutes, even seconds, after his passage the tide would have dropped so the Coast Guard couldn't pursue him over the reef. By the time the Coast Guard fell off and charted a new course around an island, the lobsterman would be unloaded and home in bed with a loyal wife who was ready to testify that he hadn't been out of the house all evening.

Such loads, run ashore in almost every cove of the state, were later moved to the cities by the bootleggers. Now and then a summer cottage would be broken into for a place to store booze until it could be moved, and somebody would find the cache and notify the police. When this happened the police liked to sit by it, waiting to arrest the bootleggers when they came to move it. But even this didn't work with a load left at South Freeport. Posting his sentinels, the sheriff patiently waited three weeks, but nobody came to get the load. Then one day there was a fire in a barn up the road, and while the sentinels ran up to help the firemen the booze disappeared.

The most notable arrest of bootleggers was made by

Chief of Police William B. Edwards of Brunswick. He had agreed to take part in a home-talent show being staged for charity by the Daughters of Isabella, and this was the night of the dress rehearsal. Chief Edwards was playing the part of Miles Standish, in a tableau depicting the conference with Massasoit. Just as the scene was deployed, Tapey Alexander came running into the theatre with the news that some booze was being landed at Mere Point. This called for the chief's immediate attention, and also that of his several officers — who were the Indians. Thus a group of rumrunners who were loading cans into a truck had the unique honor of being arrested by Miles Standish and the Wampanoag Indians, the former holding a blunderbuss and the latter in breechclouts and paint. They were the only rumrunners in the whole Volstead era who were laughing when they came to jail. There was something about the raid that amused them.

Not that arrested rumrunners ever took the formality too seriously. It was repeal, not arrest, that they feared. The high-ups were careful to send errand boys who could look clean in court. Hardly any of them had previous records, and this was to lend plausibility to their customary cry that they knew nothing about the liquor but had just chanced to be there — usually they were looking for a shore lot to buy. Something of the smooth organization behind all this was indicated by the prompt appearance of a top-grade lawyer after

each arrest, who would bring a briefcase of money and arrange bail. Then the respondent would be whisked out of the jurisdiction. These lawyers were Maine men, often from Portland. When an arrest would be made in a remote coastal town at 3:30 A.M., and a rumrunner had been in custody all of fifteen minutes, it was interesting to see a lawyer from Portland, where the banks do not stay open all night, arrive with his briefcase of money before anybody had time to take fingerprints. There was one lawyer who always had a stickpin in his necktie, which hardly seemed to prove that he dressed in haste.

Big trucks had not come into use in those days, and a favorite vehicle of the rumrunners was the Hudson Super-Six. It was heavy and could hold the unpaved roads of the time at good speed. It would also carry a considerable load in its rear seat and trunk. If, as often happened, the sheriffs took off in pursuit of one of these, there would be a merry chase o'er hill and dale until, usually, the rumrunner got away. People in the coastal towns would be awakened by the roar of passing cars, and they knew some fellow was making a getaway. Since radio was in its infancy, there was never time to set up a road block in the town ahead, and as police officers in Maine are privileged in a "hot pursuit," these chases went from jurisdiction to jurisdiction as long as they could keep the Hudson Super-Six in sight.

The Proper Time

There is the story of the rumrunner who, finally eluding his pursuers, ran low on gasoline and was delighted to see a filling station up ahead with the lights still on. He pulled in and a woman came out in a dressing gown to pump his tank full. In those days gasoline was eighteen cents a gallon, and he took fifteen gallons. When he handed the woman a twenty-dollar bill she said, "I'll have to go upstairs and get the change from my husband — he just came in, he's been out all night chasing a rumrunner."

As the rumrunner roared away he yelled at her, "Keep the change!"

But by and large, first to last, there is no great wealth of folklore in Maine out of the Volstead days. Perhaps this is because of the long-standing Maine policy of overlooking the presence of liquor in a state that isn't supposed to have any. Even today, under the strange regulations that have come out of the vote-dry-drink-wet policies, a young lady in a chain store cannot check out your six-pack of beer. She can tot up your meats and groceries, but the law says that until she becomes of age the beer is not for her to know about. She has to call over the manager, or somebody else of legal age, and a dozen customers stand in line and wait out this protection of morals. Deep in the basic nature of Maine people is an abhorrence of liquor as a public policy, and the weighty and lengthy statutes regulating the traffic must surely be a comforting sop to the popular conscience. No doubt the whole Volstead era is overlooked by Maine folklore in much the same way our legislators still believe that nobody in Maine takes a drink on the Lord's Day.

The paradox is at odds, however, with the fundamental Maine custom as expressed in the long ago by Ed Grant of Beaver Pond. Occasionally some of the "sports" would ask Mr. Grant if they might buy him a drink. Ed would push his hat back, lift his eyes in horror, throw up his hands, and rebuke them thus:

"Well, now — I suppose you know my feelings about liquor. I am not a drinking man, and while I am not intolerant of those who fancy the stuff, I do not consider the habit a good one. But ever since I was a young fellow I've noticed that if I did happen to take a drink — it was always just about now."

Prerogative

Dana Cotton, a teacher, developed an interest in Maine folklore and had a considerable collection he had gleaned up and down the state. One of his tales went like this:

He was driving along somewhere above Skowhegan, and he picked up a hitchhiker. The old fellow was wearing woodsman's clothes, carried a packsack, and seemed tired as he climbed into the automobile and thanked Dana for stopping. He didn't have much to say, even though Dana tried to encourage him to make some appropriate remarks. Then, as they went through a small village, the fellow perked up, looked at the shops and houses, and he said, "This is the place where I made my mother so ashamed."

"Ashamed?" asked Dana.

"Eyah. She was awful ashamed of me. Always said I made her a laughingstock. Not that I meant to. But I guess I did. Anyway, this is the place."

"How would you make your mother ashamed of you?" asked Dana.

"Well, she took me to a revival meeting here one time when I was a sprout in school, and I didn't behave just as she thought I should, and I heard about it for a long time. It was a real, old-fashioned, whoop-de-do revival meeting in a tent, and they had a spellbinder in the pulpit who could plaster it all over the wall. He put on a real act, and I sat there popeyed listening to him. Finally, after he got everybody worked up, he says, 'Now, I want everybody who loves the Lord Jesus to stand up!'

"So everybody in the tent stood up except me. My mother poked me, thinking maybe I had fell asleep, but I didn't get up. I wouldn't get up. She was so ashamed. She tried to pull me up, but I wouldn't get up, and then she looked around helpless with a you-know-how-kids-are expression, and it was what you might call a tight moment. But I didn't get up.

"Finally the minister says, 'Let the boy be — I'll speak to him from here!'

"So he leaned over the pulpit all friendly like, and he says, 'Young man, haven't you heard the wonderful story about the Lord Jesus?'

" 'Yes,' I says, 'I have.'

"So he says, 'Don't you believe the wonderful story about the Lord Jesus?'

"I says, 'Yes, sir, I do — I believe every word of it.'

"And he says, 'Then why don't you love the Lord Jesus?'

"I says, 'I do love the Lord Jesus.'

"So he says, 'Then why don't you stand up?'

"And I says, 'Because I don't want to.' "

Natural Question

Long ago a Mr. Ronald W. Renaldo of New Haven, Connecticut, owned a prosperous manufacturing business in that city, and the management kept a heavy strain on his mind and body. Long before the time, for

Maine was not then in the vacationland business, he would sneak away from his factory and come up here for the rest and revitalization he found in the beauty and serenity of the backwoods. At first he would come and find a room in a farmhouse, and between meals he would wander about gazing at the forest, fields and sky. But the therapeutic value of his periodic visits became so essential to him that he looked about for a piece of land he could buy and on which he could build a retreat.

He thus had a cozy cabin on the south side of North New Portland Mountain, and being a man of means he arranged that it should be looked after, cleaned, provisioned, and so on, and kept ready for his unannounced arrivals. He had a huge fireplace in the cabin, and plenty of firewood was cut for him each winter. Then when his office in New Haven began to press in on him he'd take off and come to Maine, where he'd stay until he got the kinks out of his neck, and his eyeballs stopped twitching. In his earliest comings, transportation was a problem, but after the Oakland & Bingham Railroad was laid he was in good shape — he could come right to North Anson by train and have a livery rig set him down at the end of his road up the mountain. In no time he would have his fireplace going, supper started, and the rejuvenation begun.

So, one morning in New Haven everything was ragged. It was springtime, which must never be overlooked, but it wasn't just spring fever. He tried to apply himself, but with every problem he handled ten more would line up. Then he found himself thinking about the vernal sunlight on the snowbanks of North New Portland Mountain, and the peace and quiet, and he got up and started for Maine. By the time he got off the train in North Anson he was beginning to feel a lot better. He got up on the buggy seat beside Joe Martineau (for the snow had gone until they didn't need a sleigh on the roads), and as they rode along, the indescribable beauty of the countryside filled him with joy. As they approached the end of the ride Mr. Renaldo said, "Joe, it's such a lovely day I think I'll have you set me down here and I'll walk the rest of the way."

Nothing in New Haven mattered now. Clean, fresh air, and bright sunlight over all. The hills, in particular, were breathtaking — the snow showing through the bare trunks and limbs of the hardwoods, and then the change to black spruces that seemed to be on the march and through which no snow ever showed. He came to the bridge over the river, and he leaned over the railing to look down and see how the melting snows had already begun to swell the current. Some of the ice had gone from under the bridge, and there was an arrow of black water which broke into a froth where it folded into a pool below. Along this arrow, on both sides, ice still clung to the river bankings, and Mr.

Natural Question

Renaldo was concerned to see a small boy down there playing on this ice. Not too good a place for a child to be, he thought, and then he was philosophizing about the carefree nature of youth, and here was this lad dreaming his long boyhood dreams. Sad that he must grow up and conform, and grab time by the forelock, and be hammered into a man on the clanging anvil of the workaday world. Mr. Renaldo sighed as his thoughts wandered, and he was grateful for his retreat up on the mountain, where he could come and renew himself. Where like a small boy, he thought, I can come and play. Then he was horrified to see the little boy below slip on the ice and plunge into that long arrow of black water.

In aftertimes Mr. Renaldo would try to think how he reasoned himself into action. He had never pictured himself as one to jump to motion, to rise to an occasion. It astonished him to find that he had not looked about to see if anyone were around, he had not called for help, he had not hesitated in the slightest. He ran off the bridge, hurdled the snowbanks, grabbed up a stick of some sort that lay in the cast-up debris along the riverbank, and accurately guessing everything, had been right beside the boy when he popped up at the pool. Mr. Renaldo snagged him with the stick, and he had the boy out on the ice in a twinkling. The whole thing had happened so swiftly that the boy was none the worse off, except for the intense chill of the snow water. Mr. Renaldo had scarcely stooped to look at the boy when he heard somebody call, and two men came down over the snowbanks on the run.

They said they'd seen the whole thing, and they knew who the boy was, and they'd take him where he could get warm and dry out. They picked the lad up and carried him quickly away, and Mr. Renaldo stood there alone, looking at the dark pool and all ashake to think this had happened to him. It was over so soon that it seemed not to have happened at all, and to calm his doubts Mr. Renaldo stood looking at the stick still in his hands. Then he sort of shook himself and walked back to the road and continued up to his cabin.

There he lighted his fireplace, poured himself a stout measure of strong drink, and made the lamp ready for lighting, because it would soon grow dark. He dilly-dallied with supper, for on his mind was the coincidence of his being there — if he hadn't got down from the buggy to walk the rest of the way he'd have been far beyond the bridge when the boy fell in. Then he marveled at the spontaneity of his own reactions — he hadn't gone into panic. He found himself wagging his head as he stood peeling some potatoes.

A second hooker of the intoxicant sufficed, and then supper was ready. Afterwards he sat in the big, soft armchair before the fire and tried to relax after his custom, which was what he had come to Maine to do. But he could think only of that small boy. It made Mr.

Renaldo something of a hero, really. He found himself smiling indulgently at the thought. Perhaps a Carnegie medal? The fire burned low and he added fuel. Then at last he did doze in the chair.

Somebody was knocking at his door. Somebody must have climbed the hill in the dark. He opened it, and a man and woman were standing there. "Good evening," said Mr. Renaldo.

The woman spoke. "You the man came through North New Portland this afternoon about half-past one, maybe two?"

"Yes," said Mr. Renaldo.

"The same as saw a little boy fall in the river?"

"That's right."

"And pulled him out?"

"Yes."

"Well, I'm his mother. This here is his father."

"I'm very happy to make your acquaintance," said Mr. Renaldo. "Won't you come in?"

"No, we just came up to ask. We was wondering if you chanced to notice what become of his mittens?"

His Own Grindstone

"Do you remember that old problem in the arithmetic books about a grindstone?" asked Flint Johnson one day when folklore was being swapped. "The one where Mr. A, Mr. B, and Mr. C buy a grindstone together, and the problem is to find out how much of the circumference each man must wear off to get his money's worth?"

There seemed to be general recollection of this one.

"Well," said Flint, "that's the stupidest piece of educational fiddle-faddle anybody ever cooked up. I never knew how to work the problem, but I sure knew enough to know the thing was a fake. Who in hell ever wore anything off a grindstone?"

The point was well taken. Every farm boy gets the job of turning the grindstone while his father puts an edge on axes, knives, and scythes. Then the boy grows up and he has himself a boy who cranks it until he grows up and has a boy. Generations glide by in the inexorable migrations of the years, and the grindstone sits there as good as ever, waiting for more little boys. By the time Mr. A had worn off his proper share, Eternity would be well along.

"I got a grindstone up to my place," Flint continued, "and I've used it all my life. It was an old
stone when I got it, and I came by it when I was seven
years old. By the time I got into the grade that solved
the grindstone problem I was an authority on grindstones. The teacher kept talking about Mr. A, and Mr.
B, and Mr. C, and the area of circles, and I kept trying
to set her straight about grindstones. We never had a
meeting of the minds. I suppose I'm the only boy who
ever owned his own, personal, paid-up grindstone before he went into class and met Mr. A, Mr. B, and Mr.
C, with their hypothetical supposition."

"I'm curious," said somebody. "How come you
owned your own grindstone when you were only seven
years old?"

"It does make a kind of a story," said Flint. "We
were living in Strong then, and my old man had a farm
just up the road from W. P. Littlehall, who was a
sanctimonious old bahstid with an ingrown disposition
and mean as turkey manure beer. He had the first
nickel he ever earned. The grindstone belonged to him.

"Being the kind of man he was, the boys used to
plague him. I wasn't big enough to join in the fun, but
I used to hear about the mean tricks they'd play on
W. P. Littlehall, and some of them were dandies. And
as a natural course of events, I got the idea I ought to
do something, too, so I tackled his grindstone. I sneaked
into his shed and tipped it over. It was a heavy old

thing, but I was big for my age, and after it came out of the frame I stood it up and began rolling it like a hoop. When it got momentum it went off across the dooryard and down the hill. It was comical to see it go — the handle was churning around, and it cranked all the wire off a fence as it went by. It went down almost as far as the brook, but it hit a wet spot and stopped, and there it lay with all that wire quivering. Just then old W. P. Littlehall comes out of his house and he squeaks out, 'Just what in the world do you think you're doing!' and I runs like hell.

"But he saw me good, and I hadn't been home more than three minutes when he comes charging into our yard and he pushes up to my father with his front finger wiggling at my father's nose, and he jibbers, 'Your evil boy has ruint my grindstone!' Nothing I could do but admit it, but a boy's father is always a boy's father, and my old man was rich in judgment, if nothing more. 'Now, Mr. Littlehall,' he says, 'boys will be boys, and I don't condone what he has went and did, but no need to call names and shout, and I think we can settle this in friendship. What do you suggest for punishment?' "

Flint paused, seeming to savor a fond memory, and then he went on, "Now, that was pretty sneaky of my old man. He hit the ball right at the shortstop, and old W. P. Littlehall had to field it. He lost his first mad as soon as he began reflecting on the punishment, so the rest of the meeting was simmered down. 'I think,' he said, 'that he should be made to pay for my grindstone.' 'Fair enough,' says my old man, 'I'll see that he does. Now what do you think is a fair price, and what terms can we manage?'

"By this time old W. P. Littlehall is looking a bit uncomfortable, so he says, 'It ain't the money, it's the principle of the thing. A boy has got to learn. He can't go around damaging property like that. Why don't he come and hoe corn for me until he pays for the grindstone?'

"My father says, 'Excellent! He'll be over first thing in the morning.'

"Well, I was never the greatest fancier of hoeing corn. In those days the Sandy River Valley was the sweet-corn paradise of the world. There were twenty-three corn shops within delivery distance of our farm, and of all the big corn growers in the valley, W. P. Littlehall was the biggest. He had fields that started at the road and ran back to the river. The next morning I started on one of his rows and I hoed to the river and halfway back before suppertime. Old W. P. Littlehall came down to see if I was doing a good job, and he said I was, and that he'd see me tomorrow if it didn't rain. So I went again, and I went again, and I kept going, and I liked to died in the heat and I was sick at heart for sheer lonesomeness, and in the strongest cusswords available to a seven-year-old I dressed myself down for ever touching the old fool's grindstone. My old man was no help. He'd smile and say I got myself into this, and his hands were washed. But I kept at it, and one day even old W. P. Littlehall had to give up. He came around and said I had done a fine job, and he hoped I had learned a good lesson. 'I guess you've paid for the grindstone,' he said. So I went home.

"And I got to admit the old bahstid was right. I was never so sorry for something I did. I could see that I had made a grievous error. Well, that evening after supper I went out to the barn and brought out our old horse, and I hitched her into our farm wagon. I drove her down the road to the Littlehall place, and with a couple of planks I got the grindstone up into the wagon. Old W. P. Littlehall had got it out of the swamp and back on the frame, and as I looked it over I was surprised to see that it hadn't been hurt any. According to the way he squealed, I thought I'd wrecked it. Made me a little mad to find this out. I'd hoed a lot of corn on the understanding that the grindstone had suffered considerably. Anyway, while I was loading it old W. P. Littlehall came out, and he said the same thing he'd said the other time. He said, 'Just what in the world do you think you're doing?'

"I says, 'I'm taking my grindstone home.'

" 'Your grindstone!' he says. 'That's my grindstone, and you get right down off that wagon!'

" 'No, it's my grindstone,' I says. 'I paid for it by

hoeing corn, and I've come to take it home.' So I drives along.

"Well, about the time I gets home with my grindstone, along comes old W. P. Littlehall, feather white, and he pushes up to my father again with his front finger going, and he makes an awful squeaking. My old man calms him down some, and as soon as he understands the drift he says, 'Now, Mr. Littlehall, I think you've been h'isted on your own firecracker. You called the shots, and I went along with you as a proper father should. As you said, we taught the boy a useful lesson. But now the boy has considerable logic on his side. I'm afraid he's right. He paid for the grindstone on your terms, and I'll thank you to give him a bill of sale.'

"Well, the old bahstid never gave me a bill of sale, but I kept the grindstone, and I still have it. Until he died my old man would turn and look at it every time he went by, and he'd smile to himself as if something had just struck him funny. That's the way it turned out. I owned my own grindstone when I was seven years old, and I've used it all my life, and it's just as good today as when I bought it. That's why I got into hassles with that foolish teacher. How the hell could you wear off a third of a grindstone?"

A *Variant*

Taking home the grindstone after it had been "paid for" reminds of many another Maine tale, and a single variation offered here may be sufficient example. The locale is Bangor. In the days of long pine and spruce Bangor was indeed the "Queen City," and there is no dearth of healthy stories about those times. Here the men came to frolic after their long winter in the forests, and here they congregated again in the fall to sign up for the coming season. They were rough, tough, and ready, and as Stewart Holbrook so delightfully recounted, they used to have wonderful fights just for fun. Such a funfest, in particular, took place in the Bangor House, a hostelry of that city which managed to survive the rowdydow of lumbering and remain a sedate family establishment into a newer era. On the evening in question, it being the spring of a lumbering year, the Bangor House was loaded with lumbermen who, in turn, were loaded. Such a good time was being had by all that one gentleman, fairly bubbling over with bonhomie, decided to make everything perfect by starting a fight.

Now, the company on this occasion included Warren

A Variant

Russell, a lumberman who never shirked, whether canting logs on the brow, dancing timbers down the freshets, holding up his end of the mahogany counter, obliging those who desired to fight, and so on and so forth. His great skill with the one-two was legendary, and to show his strength he had a way of grasping a hundred-pound bag of flour with his teeth and tossing it over his head. Strangely enough, while nobody could whip Mr. Russell, every so often somebody would try. If, by any prank of chance, a challenger should win, the fame of beating Mr. Russell would be immeasurable, and if, as always happened, the challenger simply got his Adam's apple kicked up through the top of his head, he merely joined that great company Mr. Russell had whipped, and this was also a kind of fame. So, on this occasion, just for fun, somebody decided to start a fight with Mr. Russell.

The fight began. And then Mr. Russell picked up his adversary and hurled him against a door. This put no great tax on Mr. Russell, but it split the door up the middle, so the owner of the Bangor House stepped forward and said, "All right, Mr. Russell, you've had your fun — now I'll thank you to pay for that door."

Being good-humored and not wishing to make himself unwelcome at the Bangor House, Mr. Russell pulled out his wallet and did so. There was some small talk to the effect that the other man really broke the door and should pay for it, but Mr. Russell said, "By no means — I had more fun than he did, and I don't want another man to pay for my pleasures." So the incident ended with good feeling all around and after a few more days the woodsmen dispersed for the summer and Bangor was quiet for a time.

That next fall Mr. Russell started for the woods, and knowing he would be more than welcome at the Bangor House he returned there and took a room. For several days the returning woodsmen renewed friendships, and the time came to board the upbound train and head for the puckerbrush.

Thus there ensued at the railway depot an interesting tableau and something of a contretemps when Mr. Russell arrived to climb into the coach with the door from the Bangor House under his arm. The conductor indicated he was not in favor of this. Being highly energized at the moment, Mr. Russell thought this was unkind and said so. His contention was that he would get on the train with his door if he'd a mind to, and he'd a mind to. At this the conductor added some asperity to his original tut-tut, and said something about calling the police. At this a group of woodsmen who were helping Mr. Russell, about a hundred and fifty in all, interposed in friendly spirit and explained the situation. Mr. Russell had paid for the door last spring, but returning this fall had found that the Bangor House had neither repaired it nor replaced it, and irked that his money had not been put to its intended use, Mr. Russell had yanked the door off its hinges and was carrying it away as his rightful possession. The plan, the men explained, was to attach it to an outhouse at Musquacook Deadwater which, heretofore lacking such a refinement, was drafty. The discussion presently convinced the conductor that he had been hasty in his judgment, and Mr. Russell carried his door into the train.

The door was used on a privy, and through the long, cold winter it constantly reminded the men of the comfort and hospitality of the Bangor House. The Bangor House, that same week, bought a new door and had it installed, and it may be seen today. Mr. Russell's door, however, and the privy as well, failed to survive the great woods fire of 1902.

Runaway's Return

Maine has undoubtedly had more than her share of boys who ran away from home. It was so easy to do — sneak aboard a vessel just before she sailed. Once under way the captain could only keep the lad for the voyage, and if the voyage lasted a couple of years the boy came home much wiser and usually had his lifetime career in hand. Indeed, many a boy who ran away to sea made out fine, and when still a young man had pile enough to retire.

Of the many stories about Maine runaways, the one selected for this compendium has to do with Roger Williams. Roger is the son of the novelist Ben Ames Williams. The Williams home was a good home, maintaining a high quality in keeping with the unusual talent who lived there, and Roger had no particular grievance which warranted his leaving. But whatever the reason that prompted him, he did run away from home according to the boyhood rules of derring-do.

Faithful to those rules, he rolled a few choice belongings together, and knowing his dear family would be distraught at bidding him farewell forever, he set off down the road without informing anybody of his intentions. Delighted with the carefree life that now surrounded him, rid of all the annoyances of close family ties, he joyed in his adventure and pressed on to seek fame and fortune.

However, he had not gone a great distance when for some reason a doubt rose in his mind, and suddenly he wasn't at all sure this was just what he wanted. There came upon him such a distinct change of attitude that he turned around and went back home. He had been away hardly more than a few brief minutes, and he walked into the kitchen to find his mother calmly wiping dishes at the sink, and his father calmly reading a newspaper by the window. His adventure had been so swift that they hadn't missed him, and he faced the ignominious realization that nobody except himself knew that he had run away from home.

In order to inform his parents, Roger would have to say something. He felt they should be informed, else they would never appreciate to the full that he had returned to their love, that he was satisfied with his lot, and that they need never worry again about his leaving. Yet as he stood there just inside the door, his father didn't look up nor did his mother turn, and the situation gave him no easy way to begin. But he had to say something.

So Roger said, "Well, I see you've still got the same old cat!"

And There She Goes!

One of the truly great pieces of folklore has been the quip, "As goes Maine so goes the Union!" An occasional authority (including the *New York Times*) has changed that to ". . . so goes the Nation," but the proper version says Union. In the days when the expression became legend a person would have said Union. The Civil War was of recent memory, and it was the Union that had been preserved. In 1875, for instance, John Abbott finished his *History of Maine,* and it was published. In conclusion he wrote, "The flood of foreign immigration is not pouring into Maine as into some other parts of the Union. But this saves the state from a vast amount of inebriation, vaga-bondage, crime, and pauperism. And those who do select Maine as their home generally come from those countries of Northern Europe where intelligence and piety prevail."

This cozy appraisal, while it serves to demonstrate the use of the word *Union* in those days, was otherwise three years off target. In 1878 Maine tackled the Greenback movement, and all pretense to intelligence, probity, sobriety, and piety collapses. No other state ever went through so much utter absurdity, or so foolishly conducted her affairs. Maine was the champ. The state simply went crazy, and stayed crazy for some time — and out of this came the Republican solidity that gave rise to "As goes Maine so goes the Union." Because it has had a political, and therefore historical, tone, folklorists have neglected it. The whole thing had to do with the resumption of specie payments, which had been suspended during the Civil War — there arose the Greenback party which opposed resumption and insisted prosperity would return only if the federal government started up the presses and printed enough paper money so everybody would be rich.

This idiocy had begun to taper off in the country at large, but in 1878 it struck Maine and entranced so many people that the Republican-Democrat situation sloughed off, and there was no majority vote for governor. This threw the election into the House of Representatives, which chose the Democrat candidate, Dr. Alonzo Garcelon. Dr. Garcelon, a medical man, took office, but he was a lot like the boy who climbed down the hole in the outhouse — he didn't know what he was getting into.

The historian's contention that Maine is peopled by intellectuals evaporated. The fallacy of the Greenback philosophy was beautifully exemplified in Maine by a farmer from up around Turner or Buckfield named Solon Chase. He would drive a yoke of oxen to the "money meetings" being held three and four a week in every community, and he would stand in the tail of his cart and make speeches on fiscal policy. "Lookit them steers!" he would shout, and then he'd tell how he paid a hundred dollars for them and they were now worth only fifty. Evidently few Mainers were intelligent enough at that time to realize that "them steers" were a perfect refutation of the whole Greenback idea. He had paid for them with inflated dollars, and now money was sound again. The steers were the same steers, but the United States dollar was twice improved. And because nobody bothered to reflect on this, Solon Chase became a great hero of the Greenbackers in Maine, and "Lookit them steers!" became a byword. Maine's great senator of the day, William Pitt Fessenden, would come home from Washington where he had been Secretary of the Treasury, and try to reason with the Greenbackers. But his experience as a money expert meant nothing to the intellectuals of Maine, and they would be rude to him and shout, "Lookit them steers!"

In those days Maine had a gubernatorial election every year. In 1879 there was again no majority for governor, but this time the Greenbackers had messed things up so there was no majority in the legislature, either. Governor Garcelon had not tried for reelection, so with some neutrality he set about lending a hand in this indecision. With his executive council he sat as a board of review, and town by town they studied the election returns to see if they could find irregularities that would change the outcome. It wasn't hard. Later the Maine Supreme Court called their irregularities "idle technicalities," but for the moment Garcelon thought he had his leverage. By a most fortuitous oddity, all the election errors had to do with Republicans! It was charged, and later proved to the court, that while Republicans were "counted out," other candidates were given time to revise errors and correct mistakes. But again, for the moment, there was the big Garcelon Count Out, and he came up with a certified legislature that had a delightfully non-Republican complexion. It was, of course, a trifle sticky, and those who were counted out refused to give up meekly. So both legislatures came to the capitol — the one that was counted out and the one that was counted in. One met by day and the other in the evening, insulting each other pleasantly, and each repealing any laws the other passed.

Governor Garcelon's term expired before anything was resolved, so he called in General Joshua L. Chamberlain, the hero of Little Round Top, and created him military governor of Maine — with orders to protect state property until a true governor should be named. Chamberlain was a fair-haired boy in Maine — he had returned famous from the battlefields and had been elected governor of Maine in 1867. His background was academic and ecclesiastical, and he afterwards became a good president of Bowdoin College. In 1879 he was commander of the state's militia, so his presence in Garcelon's cause gave some dignity to affairs. His first act was to set up a cannon on the portico of the statehouse. The portico gives on a vacant field and the west bank of the Kennebec River, beyond which are the eastern counties, so nobody knows just what General Joshua L. Chamberlain thought he was going to shoot at, but everybody felt better having him around. But with this arrangement Governor Garcelon wasn't wholly out of the picture, because by this time the Republicans had started to move the case into the court, and Garcelon had to hang around to make himself available. In effect, Maine thus had the two governors.

But the fun was just starting. In Maine the president of the senate succeeds when a governor is lacking, so Senate President Lamson now decided he should take over. The flaw in his presumption was that he was president of the old senate. But he exploited the confusion, and achieved some standing. Meantime, there were two "new" senates — the counted in and the counted out. The Republicans who had been counted out organized and then named Joseph A. Locke as their senate president. In the absence of a bona fide governor he would step up if he had been bona fide himself. Some said he was, so he, too, became a governor. "Governor" Lamson then called on everybody not to recognize "Governor" Locke, and "Governor" Locke responded with suitable remarks.

At this point, and historians seem vague as to why, Mayor Nash of the city of Augusta was asked to take over the guarding of the capitol, and he called up his city police. The militia who had been doing this under Governor Chamberlain thought the action somewhat downright, but in any event Mayor Nash seems to have had the impression that he was another governor. At one time he wouldn't let anybody in or out of the statehouse without a pass he recognized.

This gave Maine the equivalent of five concurrent

governors. But two more were yet to come. The Republican legislature, counted out but meeting anyway, held the election and named Daniel Davis governor. The Democrats and Greenbackers, as "Fusionists," did the same, and their man was Joseph Smith — not the Mormon. There was also a third legislature, never fully explained, that was meeting on pleasant days out on the lawn, but they never got anywhere and their choice for governor seems to have been lost in the crowd. The newspapers of the time hardly cast light on the dark confusion. They reported that Governor Garcelon was urging caution. Governor Chamberlain called for peace. Governor Lamson said revolutionary proceedings should not be heeded. Governor Locke demanded the surrender of the state seal. Governor Smith called up more militia, but they did not respond. Governor Davis declared an emergency. Governor Nash sent to Hallowell for more policemen.

The furor about the state was white-hot. Even ministers cried fraud, pounded their pulpits, and spoke out against the "count in" — or count out. And when Governor Chamberlain tried to bring guns and ammunition from Bangor to the capitol at Augusta, a mob surrounded the wagon on the bridge over the Kenduskeag River and threatened to topple it into the stream if it didn't turn back. The driver prudently decided to turn back since he was on the wagon at the time. Governor Garcelon knew they had him over a barrel, so he agreed to submit the matter to the supreme court.

Cagily, however, he worded a series of questions so the answers would save him a little face, but the thing had gone too far and the court couldn't let him get away with it. Instead of merely answering his questions, the court threw the whole matter open to review, and the justices unanimously held for the Republicans. There was one Democrat on the bench, and he had to go along — it was too raw even for a Democrat judge. This brought things to a head — Governor Davis sent the opinion of the court to Governor Chamberlain, Governor Chamberlain recognized Governor Davis, took his cannon, and went home. The other governors also departed, but whether abreast or single file is not stated.

The Republicans then quickly instituted two election reforms which seemed wise: two-year terms for the governor and the plurality method of election. The Greenbackers kept things stirred up for a few years, but by 1882 the Republicans had the state well in hand, and they experienced no further fundamental opposition until the days of the new-style Democrats under Franklin D. Roosevelt. And it was this solid Republican complexion of Maine, which arose from the Greenback movement, that led to the saying "As goes Maine so goes the Union." The central figure in this organization was James G. Blaine.

In those days the roster in Washington had a Maine flavor. To list a few: Elihu Washburne, Melvin Fuller, Hannibal Hamlin, Bill Frye, Lot Morrill, Bill Fessenden, Tom Reed. And James G. Blaine. All of these, one way or another, had to maintain their Washington priority by keeping things in line in their home state. The wild kicking over the traces of the Greenback movement gave the boys in Washington the heebie-jeebies of insecurity. They all hustled home to do what they could to keep the electorate in line. The one with the most tact and know-how was James G. Blaine. He and General Chamberlain were old friends — had been on the ballot together. Jim had been party to Joshua's nomination. Jim advised the Republican, rump, "counted out" legislature that finally moved the squabble before the court. Indeed, he had played a hand in the naming of certain justices, so he was able to offer discreeet suggestions that kept the court amenable. And his presence was forceful on the precinct level. Patiently, with skill, he knit things together, and out of the Greenback hullabaloo he erected a strong Republican party which hewed to his line in national affairs. Thus, guided by Jim Blaine and her other stalwarts in Washington, Maine would go to the "early bird" polls in September and pretty much reveal the national trends. It lasted long enough so the adage become folklore — "As goes Maine so goes the Union."

It seems accordingly disrespectful that folklore also includes the refrain:

> *James G. Blaine, James G. Blaine!*
> *The continental liar from the State of Maine!*

That he was also called The Plumed Knight is softening, but liar or knight, his fame depends on the peculiar intellectuality of the people of Maine, and them steers of Solon Chase.

College Physician

Although most of the Bowdoin College athletic events take place on a newer playing area, varsity football is still played on Whittier Field — one of the pleasantest facilities of its sort in any academic place. The grandstand was built before college sports became big business, but by adding bleachers Bowdoin makes do. The five acres involved might easily have been designed at the Creation for their present purpose. The flat, sandy "plains" of the region, once a public commons, made grading and leveling almost unnecessary, and the drainage is excellent. The sandy land also causes the

Pinus strobus L. to thrive, this being the eastern white pine of which Maine is so proud, and with reference to Whittier Field the "Bowdoin Pines" of which the poet Longfellow sang, " . . . that once were mine but are no longer mine." The pines fringe Whittier Field, and returning alumni may fret about Bowdoin's sometime propensities for passing when they should punt, but all of them sigh with Longfellow for the pines that were, and are, and hopefully will be. No college, anywhere, has a lovelier spot for the best man's winning. The field is named for Dr. Frank Nathaniel Whittier, college physician, Class of 1885, and this now enters the area of folklore.

When you pause to think of it, there is little folklore about the college physician. Traditionally, he is somebody who can't quite maintain a practice in Molunkus or East Overshoe and has agreed to put in his time. He has two colored pills — the red ones are for left broken legs and the blue ones are for right broken legs. He is the one who quarantined the dormitory for mumps and then found out the boy was only fat. When he writes a prescription he has to ask somebody how to spell aspirin. At Bowdoin College, however, the situation is quite otherwise — thanks in part to Dr. Frank Nathaniel Whittier.

And thanks, too, to a substantial endowment which gives the college ample funds to handle the incidence of student *malaise*. Bowdoin has a fine infirmary, so completely equipped that many small, and some large, hospitals envy her. The funds available attract more than the customary quack who, lacking a lucrative practice, finds that he can't test eyes for the State Department of Health and Welfare, and so gravitates to a collegiate sinecure. Bowdoin has always had giants, and when the present incumbent, Dr. Hanley, rises to speak in any context, the International College of Physicians and Surgeons gains stature. He moonlights as physician to the United States Olympic Team, which goes to show.

Before him there was Dr. Johnson, known as Demi-Johnson for some reason, and he was not only a gifted physician in every respect but an able and willing friend to all in the community — so much so that he could make a few personal calls and quickly settle some problem the college might otherwise have tangled with for a long time. Dr. Johnson had hardly come to Bowdoin as college physician when a smallpox epidemic hit the region, and the number of people, students and all, that he vaccinated made a useful career right there. He was preceded by Dr. Charles S. Fessenden Lincoln, an even smaller man. Dr. Lincoln had gone to the Orient as a missionary physician in his youth and distinguished himself variously, including the job as Grand Master of the Grand Masonic Lodge of China. His regalia from this preferment, when he brought it home, always interested his brethren because of the oriental symbolism — not too much like the western variety known in Maine. Because of his stature, and the size of his apron, he sometimes tripped over his lambskin when advancing to the altar, at which time Dr. Lincoln was said to "have one dragon on the ground." Dr. Lincoln passed the prime of life about the time he got into his nineties, and after that he limited himself to three sets of tennis a day, bicycle riding, and being captain of the softball team in St. Petersburg during the winter. We shall return to Dr. Lincoln after we explain about the class in hygiene.

The situation with Bowdoin, different from any other Maine college in this respect, arises from the fact that the Maine Medical School was on that campus. When wisdom suggested closing the school, since it was nowhere near a hospital or medical center, Bowdoin inherited the assets, which included a substantial alumni body of medical men. This affinity didn't peter out because the endowment funds of the old medical school were at the disposal of the college, and Bowdoin was still able to finance students liberally. All medical schools continue to respect Bowdoin, not alone for the quality of the men she sends into the profession, but because she is able to pay some of their bills. In short, Bowdoin's alumni list is more than larded with "M.D." When, to this backlog, was added a generous bequest to erect and maintain a splendid infirmary, staff it, equip it, and provide peripheral services, Bowdoin was able to attract the kind of superior man she has.

An incident of some years back points this up. In a football game on Whittier Field a luckless halfback on the Bowdoin squad got creamed by a half-dozen hog callers from the University of Maine, and nobody needed to be a physician to understand what happened. The crack of his leg bone came across the field like a pistol shot. Even though it was in the first quarter of the game, a great many people in the stands were seen to rise and leave as the young man was carried off on a stretcher. About every fourth man at the game was a doctor, and he hastened to the infirmary to see if he might be of assistance.

It takes four or five minutes to walk from Whittier Field to the infirmary, and in that time the front entry was clogged with Bowdoin doctors trying to get in. No broken leg in the history of athletics was ever attended by such a conclave of experts. One surgeon, trying to get inside, was heard to call out, "Is there an ostiary in the crowd?" The injured student, or halfback, had ten anesthetists, and beyond them, row on row, he could see the bone specialists arriving to tell the thirty-four radiologists just what they wanted for pictures. The student was trying to tell somebody to get a guest book and have it signed when he went out like a light.

Dr. Whittier, the pacemaker for the position of Bowdoin physician, arose from this interesting situation. With his baccalaureate and master's from the college, he had his medical degree from the school, and he was to receive also an honorary doctorate in the twilight of his career, in 1924. He studied in London and in Berlin, and returned to his alma mater to instruct. He was professor of pathology and bacteriology. He also directed the gymnasium and physical training. In stature he was a gaunt, gangling man, whose swinging gait across campus is still recalled and mentioned by the Old Guard alumni — the only ones who now remember him. He was a character, a gentleman, a scholar, a physician, a friend, and all else that distinguishes a man and places him above others.

And in the general pattern of college affairs it befell that Dr. Whittier taught a special class. It was known as Hygiene, and it was designed to spend some of the surplus income the institution couldn't otherwise properly apply to other medical affairs. The course was required, but there is no record of outstanding failures. It began with basic anatomy and physiology, and continued into hygiene, where candidates for a degree were instructed in the care of the fingernails, and so on, and exhorted to be cleanly. It never became a course that positively required a teacher of Dr. Whittier's standing, but he conducted it with dignity. What it lacked in scholastic merit it gained in giving all Bowdoin students that much of Dr. Whittier's time and presence. By the use of its "medical" funds the college provided free textbooks for Hygiene — the only class and course of which this was so. After Dr. Whittier ceased to conduct it, and Dr. Lincoln came, the class had its name changed, but not officially. Because of Dr. Lincoln's happy custom of illustrating his points with off-color jokes, the students began calling it, "Smutty Stories, 1–2."

All of which is pertinent and important, because from Dr. Whittier's class in hygiene came a nugget of Bowdoin folklore which is probably unique in this field. With so much to draw from, it is curious that more did not be remembered about the college physicians.

When Dr. Whittier began teaching this hygiene course, he brought a great dictionary stand into the classroom, and upon it he placed a huge pulpit Bible. Then, to give his lectures the dignity he desired, he commenced every class by reading one verse from the Bible. Whether this had any spiritual value was never accurately revealed in any surveys or statistics, but it did serve the purposes of quieting the scuffling, bringing each man to attention, and establishing a mood. When the first class assembled in the fall, Dr. Whittier would intone, "In the beginning, God created the Heaven and the Earth . . ." and afterward, day to day, he would read a verse, until at the end of the semester he was wherever it took him. Each time he began with a new class he would start in the beginning.

He began this in 1891, and in 1924 was still teaching the same class and reading from the same Bible, so the matter had become well established as a fine old Bowdoin tradition — of which the institution has had no lack. And it so happened that one year, when the tradition was old, a couple of boys sneaked into the classroom one day before Dr. Whittier arrived, and they pasted two sheets of the Bible together.

It was some time before Dr. Whittier, reading one verse at a time, came to these two pasted pages. But eventually he did, and he stepped to the stand and began reading:

"Now Ahab betook himself to a far country, and there he took unto himself a wife, and she . . ."

Now he turns the page.

". . . and she — was forty cubits in breadth, an hundred cubits in length, and had ribs of oak."

Dr. Whittier's lean face gave no indication that he was surprised. He turned the page back and began again:

"Now Ahab betook himself to a far country, and there he took unto himself a wife, and she . . ."

He turns the page again.

". . . and she — was forty cubits in breadth, an hundred cubits in length, and had ribs of oak."

He closed the Bible. "Gentlemen," he said, for this was the correct way to address a class at Bowdoin until coeducation was recently consummated, "Gentlemen," he said, "I do not recall encountering this particular passage before, but truly — the woman was well built."

Diagnosis

Caught up in the fervor that ferved at the beginning of the American Civil War, Richard M. Barter of Litchfield, fifteen years old, volunteered for service in the 16th Maine Regiment. He was large for his age, and a very smart and able young man, but he was naive and countrified. He showed up for mustering in homespun trousers, doeskin jacket tied around with thongs, Indian moccasins, and a beaverskin cap easily worth more in the going market than all the other caps of the regiment put together. When he was instructed to strip and don the official uniform, his comrades were truly surprised to see that he didn't know how to lace a pair of boots, button his shirt, and fasten his pants. This promoted interest in the lad, and he became the regimental favorite. Thus there developed much concern when he shortly complained that he wasn't feeling tiptop, and something he couldn't seem to understand made him feel indisposed.

The regimental surgeon, a Dr. Thaddeus Spofford of

Richmond, gave the boy a routine examination but could find nothing wrong. Richard said that he had a constant ringing in his ears and a dull, disconcerting pressure at the nape of his neck, something that had never bothered him back on the farm in Litchfield and which he couldn't explain. Dr. Spofford would readily have believed the boy was goldbricking, except that he insisted on standing his watch, falling in, and doing everything expected of a good soldier in spite of his discomfort. The boy kept apologizing, and insisted he would be "all right," and yet he looked more wan and haggard with each passing day and continued to complain about the noises in his ears and the heaviness on his neck. Dr. Spofford kept an eye on the boy, and finally convinced he was not putting on an act, had him transferred to a hospital, where more experienced physicians could give him a look.

Ordered to bed and subjected to much examination, Richard was unhappy. It was his place, he said, to be with his regiment and his comrades, and while he had endured this unexplained sensation, he was glad to do so for patriotic reasons. He would prefer, he repeated, to be with the troops. But Dr. Spofford was an able man, and since he had sent this patient in for care the other doctors wanted to do all they could. They kept young Richard in bed almost two weeks and repeatedly returned to him to look him all over again. There was nothing, they concluded, that should cause this mysterious sensation. Psychology, at that time, was hardly rampant, so they could not phrase their thoughts accordingly, but they agreed that this was all in the boy's head, and that in spite of his insistence that he should be with the soldiers, this was a deep-seated device to effect the opposite. Indeed, their opinion was corroborated by the fact that once Richard was put to bed, his discomfort passed, and all during his stay in the hospital he had felt no ringing in his ears and no depression at his neck. He was accordingly discharged from the hospital and sent to the quartermaster corps to be given a new uniform so he could return to active duty.

The supply sergeant fitted him out, and said, "What size shirt do you take?"

Richard said, "Fourteen and a half."

"You sure?"

"Yes. Truth is, Mr. Sergeant, I ain't never wore no shirt until I joined the soldiers, but in Augusty, when I was mustered in, they give me a fourteen and a half."

"Seems small."

"I don't know about that. But it was a fourteen and a half."

"All right, if you say so. I'll give you a fourteen and a half. But I'll bet it'll be so tight you'll have a ringing in your ears, and the back of your neck will feel like it was in a bear trap."

Non Sequitur Sed Seq.

The geology of Maine is a hodgepodge that constantly amazes its students. A broken crystal of tourmaline may turn up in two pieces a hundred miles apart, each buried in its own ancient layer. Howard Irish, who owned Mt. Micah and mined its tumbled strata once said, "We've found everything here except *mirabile dictu,* and yesterday I found that." So it runs with folklore. When Jimmie Asworth was telling how he got stuck in an elevator in the old Falmouth Hotel in Portland, Buzz Randall said, "That reminds me of one spring on the Allagash . . ."

Somebody asked how getting stuck in a hotel elevator would remind of the Allagash, and Buzz said, "I had to get into my yarn somehow."

It may therefore be interesting to folklore students to sample several selections which came out of one studious session, each "reminded" by another, and in this way they can understand how, like the minerals of Mt. Micah, the jewels turn up in implausible sequence.

Dr. Armand Albert of Van Buren came of ancient Acadian stock, and studied medicine at Laval University in Quebec. He had never heard any English until he was a doctor of medicine, and all his life he was called Al-bear, not Al-bert. He came down into the St. John Valley, which is the boundary between northern Maine and Canada, and set up his practice. Van Buren is a Maine town, and across the river is St. Leonard in Quebec, so that to serve this international community Dr. Albert needed two licenses. His license to practice in "The British Empire" was already in hand, and some may consider that a substantial franchise, but it was no good in Van Buren. Dr. Albert came down to the state capitol at Augusta and took his state board tests to get his license to practice in Maine. He came through with flying colors, but after it was over one of the examining physicians heard that Dr. Albert spoke no English. He quickly found an interpreter, and he said, "Tell Dr. Albert that if he had only told us, we would have prepared his examination in French."

Dr. Albert answered, "Tell him it makes no difference — I have Latin."

The St. John Valley is basically French — but not the Quebec branch. In the *Evangeline* story, when the refugees from Grand Pré headed for Louisiana, not all made that long trip. A great many merely moved up the St. John River into the Maine-Quebec wilderness, and they have been there ever since. They were there long before English-speaking settlers moved into the region. Many of them still speak French exclusively, and it is an interesting, exciting French, which broke off from the mother tongue three centuries ago. No people in all the world are as proud of their heritage as the Acadians — Acadie being the French name for Nova Scotia. In the St. John Valley the Scotch-English-Irish are come-latelies; the Quebec *habitant* is unimpressive. If you can say, *"Mais non, monsieur, pas moi — je suis acadien!"* you are the elite. Dr. Albert was sentient of all this, and he carried himself as a gentleman of the true definition — *"celui qui ne se pique de rien."* As a physician he delivered babies, plucked splinters, attended the aged, and made tortuous treks on snowshoes to outlying farms. He was beloved and respected, and knew excellent well that people found him more available than God and frequently of more immediate help. He was wise, and he was well read. He was somewhat roly-poly, and perhaps never looked like a physician. But he tied his own flies, was famous for his *perdrix en chou,* and he could smoke a *truite* so you wouldn't believe it. There was little Dr. Albert hadn't turned his hand to in his constant study of affairs and their causes, and a patient might interrupt him as he was making his spaghetti sauce or as he was rebuilding the motor in his automobile. *"Ça va,"* he'd say.

His stories went on and on. Once he was called to deliver a baby over in St. Leonard, so he cranked his battered jalopy, picked up the woman who helped him as midwife, and bounced to the scene. When he lifted the sheet on the bed to examine the woman he was amazed to discover that her abdominal hair was peroxide-bleached until it looked like something you might see in Sweden. Dr. Albert quickly looked at the woman's head, where he saw a pair of black eyes, dark skin, and the straight, black hair of a good St. John *bonne femme.* He smiled, and to the midwife he said, "We must write this up for the medical journal — a two-toned mother!"

The patient said, "But I did it, Doctor, just for you!"

Another of his stories was about a delivery when he arrived much too early. Since it was snowing and he was far out of town he decided to wait, so he sat in a rocking chair by the kitchen window and soon fell asleep. When he woke up he was in the woman's bed in the bedroom, and she was sitting up in the rocking chair. They had only the one bed in the house, and they were ashamed that the good physician should sleep sitting up. He roused, got the woman back in bed, and soon had his work done.

The greatest thing that ever happened to Dr. Armand Albert was his election as president of the Maine Medical Society. It was the supreme honor for any doctor, but to the little backcountry physician of distant St. John Valley it was beyond his comprehension. The great surgeons downstate had properly recognized the devotion and dedication, the skill and genius, of the man, but to him it didn't make sense. However, having been thus honored, he decided to give it his all. The Maine Medical Society never had a president who worked harder at it. And among other things, he drove his battered old automobile down to Bangor and swapped it in on a Cadillac — he wanted something that befitted his position. They didn't allow him much on his ancient model, which knew every mudhole and snowbank in the valley, but he didn't care. He started back for Van Buren in his beautiful new automobile, and he got almost into Lincoln before he remembered that he had forgotten his spittoon. Dr. Albert always had a cuspidor on the floor of his car, right beside him, and suddenly he had a need for it and it wasn't there. He turned back to Bangor to get the receptacle out of his old machine, and after installing it fondly in his new Cadillac, he set out once more for Van Buren.

His term of office was a complete delight for all. He came in his handsome Cadillac to all the county meetings. He attended Cancer Crusade, Heart Fund, and March of Dimes and ate the lasagne luncheons. The state convention was a tremendous success. His bubbling, warm, Gallic personality was like an infusion, and physicians and surgeons who had never heard of Dr. Albert, or Van Buren for that matter, sang his praises and marveled at the wonderful job he was doing as president. He, in turn, was overjoyed to have this preferment settle upon an obscure *médecin,* and the people of Van Buren and St. Leonard made him tell of his wonderful experiences when he went down to Waterville, Bangor, Portland, Lewiston, to address the meetings.

It was, all the same, something of a surprise when he learned that being president meant that he must attend the national convocation of the American Medical Society. That this was to be in Chicago frightened him — it was such a distance, and such a great city. But an honor was an honor, and this he would do. So when the time came he installed his very lovely wife Marie, a true patrician from the old stock of Quebec City, in the great, shining Cadillac, and they set out. Naturally, they took the route via St. Leonard, and they paused in Montreal, Ottawa, and Toronto. Their Canadian origins would make them feel at home in these cities, and it would condition them for the traffic in Chicago.

In Chicago they had little trouble finding the hotel where the convention was taking place, and Dr. Albert noticed that the doorman gave his vehicle an approving survey as it came to a stop. He might be the little country doctor from the backwoods of Maine, but he had arrived in style.

The doorman opened the door for Mrs. Albert, leaned down, and said, "Welcome to Chicago, Dr. Albert!"

"Now wait a minute," said Dr. Albert. "I've never been here; you don't know me; how do you call me by name?"

"I was told to look for a spittoon."

This, a student will see, very properly reminds somebody else of another story, which is a recitation by a boat builder of Southport Island, who is telling of something that happened:

"I was all drove up, shop full of things to do, and busy thirty-six hours a day, and they come in and they says, 'You got to make a casket for Ben.' Well, as I say, I had boats to build, boats to fix, boats to make over, boats to paint, boats to rig, and all the other kind of boats, and the last thing I wanted to do was stop and build somebody a casket, even though it was for Ben, although ordinarily I'd-a been glad to, because he was a friend of mine.

"So I says, 'No, I'm right out straight here with boats, and I got no time to make nobody no caskets. I can't. You got to find somebody else.'

"They said, 'You got to do it — he was your best friend.' I said, 'It don't make no odds, a man can only do so much, and I got enough work promised so I'll never catch up. You go find somebody else.'

"So they slaps a ten-dollar bill on the bench, and they says, 'Now — will you make Ben's casket?' Of course, ten dollars was a good price for a casket in them days, and I suppose they thought it would tease

me, but I says, 'No — money ain't the object; it's strictly a matter of time. I just ain't got the time.'

"So then they brings out a quart of whiskey, and they stood that on top of the ten-dollar bill, and they said, 'Now — will you make Ben's casket?'

"I says, 'Boys, you've just persuaded me.' So I cleared off a place and began to lay out some lumber, and I had to move the bottle, so I thought I'd see what it was like, and I took a sip. It was good. Very good. And I went to work, and I guess I sipped now and then, because the next thing I knew I was sitting on that nail keg over there, and they was shaking me, and they was saying, 'Wake up, wake up — did you finish Ben's casket?'

"So I says, 'Yes, I did — it's right over there on the end bench. Ain't she a beauty?' So they went over and looked at it, and one of them says, 'What's this thing here?'

"Well, I went over to see what he was pointing at, and I never felt so foolish in my life. Foolishest thing I ever did — be damned if I hadn't gone and put a centerboard to her!'"

Which in turn, like the tourmaline crystal, reminded of the time Pokey Hubbard shipped eels. Pokey set eel pots in the river below the falls at Brunswick, and every evening he'd bring a barrel of eels up in a wagon and put them on the train for New York. In those days every through train had a fish car that was going to the

Fulton Fish Market. It would gather in the odds and ends of the coastal fisheries for the peculiar purposes of the Fulton — winkles, urchins, and things like that, and Pokey's barrel of eels. Eels are durable, and while most forms of piscatorial provender perish and become passive, eels do not. You can cooper them in a barrel in Brunswick, and they will swirl themselves around in the barrel all the way to New York.

So on one particular evening Brunswick was the scene of a scintillating event. The new Masonic Lodge rooms were to be dedicated, and to do the thing with official hand the Grand Master of the Grand Lodge of Maine, attended by his suite and retinue, was coming on the evening train. The sumptuous banquet would be followed by appropriate exercises, all in due form. The train ground to a stop at the depot, and while Pokey was putting his barrel of eels on the front end, the Grand Master and his attendants were getting off at the other. Preceded by the Grand Wardens and supported by the Grand Deacons, the Grand Master drew himself up in array on the platform. Meantime, to receive him, the Master and Wardens of the Brunswick lodge had taken a position of welcome and were standing at attention. The Marshal was about to step forward and commence the amenities. It was, truly, a magnificent sight to see, and not only all the other passengers, but a good group of bystanders were giving it their attention.

And it must have been that Pokey gave it his attention, too, because he lost control of his barrel and it
fell to the platform and smashed. A good assortment
of the eels went one way, but just as many went the
other and joined the fraternity of Ancient Free and
Accepted Masons, but not according to the ancient
usages and customs of the order.

Sad Outcome

Away down east in the town of Danforth they used to
have a small jest they'd pull on any traveling salesman
who happened to fit into the pattern, and it turned
many of them into an upright life of rectified sobriety.
Things revolved around the low quality of the local
booze — it was cheap and nourishing, but created a
chemical reaction that left the unaccustomed partici-
pant weak and wobbly. It did not, however, have any
particular effect on those who had, by constant use,
become acquainted with it. The stuff was made in the
rear of a blacksmith shop by Russell Howard, and try
as he might, Russell couldn't seem to master some of
the refinement problems. Anybody who took any for
the first time would be sick as a dog for three days.

But the three conspirators in this Danforth jest, Jim,

Dudley, and Brad, had long since developed an immunity, and they could pursue this rotgut without complications — all they needed was somebody to keep them supplied. Jim, Dudley, and Brad, being male, unwed, unattached, and so disposed, had rooms at the Henshaw House, which was the inn in old-time Danforth and the only accommodations for wayfarers. Traveling salesmen, always known as drummers in those days, used it if perverse fate caused them to dally in Danforth. Any such traveling salesman would find Jim, Dudley, and Brad shooting fifteen-ball pool in the lobby after supper.

The affable manner in which this trio greeted and fraternized with such a salesman always gave him a cozy feeling about the good people of Danforth, and after a few rounds of pool such a salesman would be further delighted to find he had been invited to play some cards — the game usually taking place in the salesman's room. The pattern of these encounters was almost routine, but Jim, Dudley, and Brad were able to guide it if needed. Hardly ever did they sit down to deal but the salesman would apologize that he had nothing to offer in the way of a drink, and if he didn't Jim, Dudley, and Brad would cause him to come to it. One thing led to another, until it was made known that a drink could be had if application were made to Russell Howard. Pleased to have company for the evening, and cheered by the friendliness of Jim, Dudley, and Brad, the salesman would haul out his wallet and offer to finance such an expedition, whereat Jim, Dudley, and Brad would flip coins, odd man to go for the booze.

In this way a good time was had by all, and the salesman would drink up just as hearty as anybody. At a Christian hour the group would disband.

The next morning the salesman would wake up with a head like a bushel basket and feel around at arm's length for his ears. He would be dizzy, his throat would be inflamed, and he would have pains in his chest. In addition, his system would be unsynchronized, making breakfast impossible, and he soon discovered other difficulties which grew worse as he went along. Having a schedule and appointments, he had to go along, and through Calais and Eastport, and up into Aroostook County, as he made his calls, he wondered if he would last out the trip. He always did, as Russell Howard's liquor was not really lethal.

Now Jim, Dudley, and Brad were mighty careful to keep a good memory about those salesmen they had played cards with, and when one of them would, as many did, return to the Henshaw House, they had a discreet way of handling him. It was their practice to receive him singly. That is, two of them would fail to appear, and the third would saunter into the lobby to greet the victim. It would be, say, Brad, and Brad would pump the fellow's hand and say he was glad to see him again.

Shortly, of course, the drummer would ask if Brad had experienced any ill effects after that night they had played cards, and Brad would say, "Some, yes — I felt mean the next day. But at least we had something to drink, and in Maine that's living!"

And then the drummer would naturally inquire for Jim and Dudley.

"Them? Oh, they both died the morning after you was here."

Areopagitica

One great piece of Maine folklore has long served as a stopper for that great menace to truth and reliability — the Texan. The essential difference between Texas and Maine is that between the wild roar of the wind in a storm and the tender whisper in one's beloved's ear. For every Texan who has the biggest, the best, the richest, the deepest, the longest, there is a quiet Maine retort which reduces the bombast to nothing. And this story of the poker game in Mars Hill has long been used to silence the loud, bragging Texan whenever somebody from the Pine Tree State thinks he needs chastising.

In essence, it is the refined version of the simple topper. In a basic form, it runs like this: One man is bragging about the size of the vegetables he grows on his farm. He describes a cabbage they grew which broke the scales at the haymarket and could be moved only with heavy equipment. When he is finished somebody will quietly say, "We never grew nothing as big as that up around where I come from. Biggest thing I ever remember was the pot my father made. He had a stove foundry, and just for fun one time he decided to cast an oversize iron pot. I don't truthfully recall just how big it was, but I know it was so far across the mouth of it that if the man on one edge wanted to talk to the man on the other, they had to have a third man in the middle to relay the conversation. They said the bail on the thing used as much iron as you'd use for thirty freight cars. It was a big pot, anyway, and it came in mighty handy."

"Handy?" says the first man. "What would anybody use a pot as big as that for?"

"To cook them damn cabbages you grow over to your place."

A slightly more refined version runs: Two men were fishing on opposite shores of a stream, far enough apart so they had to shout at each other.

"You caught anything?" one of them yells.

"I just pulled in a bass four feet long!" is the answer, and then, "How about you?"

"I just caught a lantern I lost overboard three years ago, and it's still lit!"

Silence for a moment, and then, "Tell you what I'll do — I'll take three feet off my bass if you'll blow out that damn light!"

In this context there thus developed in northern Maine the topper for the Texan, and unlike Texas tales this one is based on a verifiable fact — the perennial poker game. The locale is Mars Hill, a town in Aroostook County, bordering New Brunswick, where few of today's inhabitants seem to know just how their community got its name. Just east'ard of the village, an important potato center, there is a mountain. Today it has a ski slope. It is said to be the first point in the United States to receive the rays of the rising sun. Clearly, some Bible student among the original settlers whimsically named it for the Hill of Ares outside Attic Athens where the tribunal met and where St. Paul addressed the Athenians. A nice little touch, and one that should be better understood by Aroostookians. The village, of course, took its name from the mountain. So nobody knows just when it started, but long ago in the beginnings of the great Maine potato business a poker game in one of the potato houses became everlasting. It has never stopped.

Students unfamiliar with Maine potato houses will

need some explanation. After the harvest, it grows cold in Aroostook, and the potatoes must be stored where they will not freeze. Shipment to market is made throughout the winter, and besides storage space the potato house will have room for grading and packing. Such a storage building is built mostly below ground, like a cellar, with only the roof and the door end exposed. It will have a heater of some sort that can be started up when the winter gets cold enough to work inside and threaten the potatoes. Naturally, somebody must attend all this constantly because the potatoes in storage are numerous and valuable. Sitting around with a bunch of potatoes isn't much fun, so the idea of the poker game was to cheat the tedium.

A potato cellar is not much on style. The game goes on around the top of a potato barrel, with a few stools and boxes to sit on, and a single light bulb hangs by its own cord from the roof rafters high overhead. Sometimes a numerous group plays, at which time the top of the barrel is scarcely large enough, but at other times the attendance will drop to a trio. But day or night, year in and year out, as somebody leaves somebody else will arrive, and the game is a century old.

So, one year a wealthy Texan, having little else to do but amuse himself, called in his pilot and said, "Tomorrow I'm going up to the Miramichi for the salmon fishing." This he did, and because no proper salmon would dare not bite a Texan's lure, he had himself a merry time and was at last ready to be flown home. He had suitably impressed the guides, camp operators, and sundry New Brunswickers of the charms and superiority of Texas, so there was no reason to linger longer. His pilot revved up and took off.

But the return flight to Texas had hardly begun when the motor swallowed a valve and the pilot had to come down in the first level place he could find. He barely skimmed the top of Mars Hill and made a perfect landing in a potato field just outside the community of the same name. A farmer came over and wanted to know if there was anything he could do, and thus this Texan was stuck in Mars Hill while his pilot waited for repair parts and rebuilt the motor.

Those not to the Mars Hill situation born, or naturalized, would then, and do now, consider the place somewhat meager in its entertainment opportunities. The Texan, although he was sheltered and comfortable, and the hospitality was the usual unstinting Aroostook kind, found the days dreary, the evenings long, and the morrows uninviting. There was nothing to do. It was several days before somebody, trying to aid in his amusement, thought of the poker game. The Texan was asked, "Would you like to play some poker?"

"Poker," said the Texan, "is my meat and drink. I'm the best poker player in Texas, where the game was invented. I would rather play poker than eat. Lead me to it!"

"Well," the fellow says, "I don't have no right to invite you in, but I doubt if the boys would mind, seeing as you're stuck like this. I'll take you over, and least we can do is ask."

So the Texan arrives at the potato house, and he is disappointed in the rustic appearance of the place: the barrel, boxes and stools, the little light bulb, and the lanky Maine potato farmers sitting in dirt-crusted overalls. It is not his idea of how things should be done. But boredom had been unbearable, and at least this was something to do. "Do you mind if I sit in?" he boomed out heartily, in his best hooraw manner. Everybody turned to look at him, and somebody said, "No, of course not. Pull up a box."

"Fine, fine!" said the Texan. "Mighty glad to find something to do in this jumping-off place. Thanks for inviting me."

So he hitched up a box, and they moved around to make room for him, and he pulled out his wallet. He leaned on the barrel to see just who was the banker, and he said, "Give me a thousand dollars worth of chips!"

So they gave him a blue chip.

Tie and Jacket

The building collapsed long ago and puckerbrush has taken over, but if you know where to look you can still see a bit of the foundation. It used to be a little roadside restaurant far down in Washington County. It snagged a few summer tourists in season, so the cook, who owned the place, would hire a college boy to act as doorman, headwaiter, and cashier. He wore a bow tie and gave the dining room a little class. So one day the place was fairly well filled with seasonal trade — although being full it still didn't hold many — and a homespun character in faded overalls and pea smock got out of a battered pickup truck and started in. The college boy met him at the door.

"I'm sorry," he said, "we insist on tie and jacket in the dining room."

"So what is that supposed to mean?"

"Merely, sir, that we do have a particular clientele. No offense, and we are not formal, but we like to keep neat."

"Is that so?" said the man. "Who owns this place?"

"The proprietor is Mr. Randall, sir. He's also the chef. He's in the kitchen."

[147]

So the homespun character in faded overalls and pea smock went around to the back door, and he stuck his head in and said, "Your name Randall?"

"That's me!"

"How much do you want for this place?"

After the homespun character had bought and paid for the restaurant he folded the bill of sale into his wallet and went around front, where he fired the college boy and then had a good dinner. He did not, of course, pay for it, and then he got in his truck and drove off and nobody thereabouts has seen him since. Mr. Randall didn't know just what to do. The place was just the same, but it wasn't Mr. Randall's any more. He finally took the money he got for it and built a new restaurant in a better location and stayed in business.

You have now been introduced to the Jordan boys. Almost every Maine town has had their like, usually in the singular, but in this instance they were brothers. Smart, handy, hard-working, astute, and willing to play the long pull, they became wealthy, even though wealth was hardly their aim. The Jordan boys were named Solomon and Hiram, contracted to Sollie and Hi, and when they were in their eighties they were still called the "boys." In the twilight of their lives they could put their hands on more money than anybody else in town, but they still cleaned their own septic tanks and split their own wood. Neither, lifetime long, had ever done anything without first consulting the other, and whatever they undertook they stood there side by side, doing the work and sharing in the gain. Neither had any extended formal education, but universities could pool their faculties and never come up with half the Jordan boys knew. On that day in Washington County, after conferring with Hi, Sollie had struck out to buy a sawmill they heard was for sale, and he had so much money with him that a small restaurant was nothing.

When they were boys, the essence of good husbandry was taught them by a long winter when they had precious little to eat. Their father, a farmer, did well, but those were other times and money was something nobody saw much of. One year the father planted ten acres of rutabaga turnips, and as the summer progressed this looked like a sound investment. The two youngsters, Sollie and Hi, were kept hoeing and cultivating, and by the time the first September frost struck, the field was handsome. Their father was pleased, and while he wasn't one to blab all the time, he did compliment them on their work and say they had grown the finest piece of turnips he ever clapped an eye to. Turnips attain their flavor in late season, and are best if left in the ground right to freeze-up. So the weather was already cold when Mr. Jordan set his boys to harvesting the field — and this is hard work. Each turnip must be pulled, have its top slashed off with a knife, its dirt rubbed off, and then be piled in the cart. They had a one-horse farm wagon and a patient old plug who stood for them and would move ahead on command without need of touching the reins. When the boys had the cart filled they would bring the load to the house and lug the turnips down cellar to be piled in bins for storage. So this job went on day after day, and there was no problem about school because in those times the winter term didn't commence until all crops were in. And child labor wasn't exploited — it was a way of life.

Thus the days came when the boys were tired of turnips. And as they were pulling and cutting in the field they looked up and saw Reid Edgecomb coming along the road with a droopy team of horses and an empty cart. Reid, well known to the boys, pulled up and remarked on what a fine field of turnips this was. They thanked him, and one thing led to another until Sollie said, "Would you like some?" Reid opined that he didn't know but what he would, so he descended to throw a few on, and Sollie said, "Take all you want — the more you take the fewer we have to haul home, and Lord knows we got enough." So it was, and Reid took a load home, and then he came back and got some more, and Father Jordan didn't know a thing about this. The boys would haul a load and Reid would haul a load. One time Reid had so many turnips in his cart that his droopy horses couldn't start the load in the soft ground, so the boys hitched their nag on ahead and got him going. But one day the piece was harvested, and Father Jordan turned a flock of hogs into it to clean up the skips.

Winter descended and the snows came. And one day Father Jordan said, "Well, I guess it's about the right time to commence moving a few turnips." So he hitched the team, filled the sled box with bags of turnips, set two lighted lanterns under blankets to keep things from freezing, and struck off to visit the stores. Late that afternoon he came home tired and perplexed.

"I couldn't sell a turnip," he said. "Everybody's got turnips. They said Reid Edgecomb had been bringing in some fine turnips that they like, and they were satisfied and didn't care to change. I didn't know Reid Edgecomb grew any turnips this year. Did you, boys?"

"No," said Sollie.

"No," said Hi.

So for want of money that would have come from turnips, the Jordan family had a lean winter, and many a night Sollie and Hi went to bed with mighty little in their stomachs. They never again were known to give anything away.

In later times they had a garage that served as head-quarters for their many activities, and when they realized the future was all ahead of them they signed up to be the Ford agency. They did fine selling the

Model T, and as they were good mechanics they could do repairs and keep customers happy. Then one day Ford came out with a dubious contrivance which was called a Fordson. It was a farm tractor, prophetic and ahead of its time. It had more bugs than a year-old pine log. For one thing, it would climb up on torque and tip back on the driver. Possibly it worked fine in prairie country, but in hilly Maine it was a threat. Nor were farmers yet convinced that a tractor was the thing to have, and there was great sales resistance. Perhaps because of this, Ford shipped a carload of these things to every dealer on a "must" basis, and to Sollie and Hi this was a great surprise. The freight car arrived on the siding and Sollie and Hi had to go to the bank and fix up a sight draft to cover the bill of lading before they could see what they'd bought — and they were unhappy. It was years before they got rid of the last one, and months between every sale. One day Hi came into the garage and announced that he had succeeded in selling another one.

"Did we make?" asked Sollie.

"Well, I don't rightly know yet. Roy Thayer made me an offer, and I took it. He offered two cows, one fresh and one due, a lawn mower, two hives of bees, a hundredweight of yellow-eye beans, a Buckeye mower with a broken pitman, five pounds of butter, and a lot in the cemetery."

"Holy old MacIntosh!" said Sollie.

"I swapped the mower to Puskie Dunlap for a manure spreader, and I worked the spreader off on Lem Mathews for eighteen dollars. Jim Lunt gave me two dollars for the lawn mower. Herman Andresen gave me ten dollars for the bees. Marchak & Lowery has the beans in the store and will pay what they get, less two cents a pound. The cows I had trouble with. I got seventy-five from Hazzie Buker for the milker, and Tom Mosher took the other one for eighty-two-fifty. But it took a lot of time. The butter I took myself, figuring thirty cents a pound. And I'm pooped. I never done such a day's work in my life."

"Sounds so," said Sollie. "But what do you figure we made out of all this?"

"A lot in the cemetery, and I'll toss you for it."

One year Sollie and Hi contracted to plow snow for several towns in the area. They had some old trucks with blades on front, and they bid the work off at so much per mile per storm. They did fine until February, when a no'theaster settled in and blew snow for a week. The Jordan boys didn't have anything that would touch snow like that, and everybody was clamoring to have his road broken. There was a penalty clause in the contract, so something had to be done. They consulted, and Sollie took the next train to Boston.

He arrived at the salesroom of a heavy equipment agency out on Commonwealth Avenue and came in to bend and sniff the rose in a vase on the receptionist's desk. She surveyed him in some dismay. Overalls smeared with spruce pitch, gear grease, and other rural decorations, tucked into lumberman's felt boots and rubbers. A wide-collared mackinaw in green and black check, also liberally adorned as beforesaid. Three days of beard. A Scotch woodsman's cap, with the ear-flappers tied up. And a pair of doubleknit mittens caught up under one arm. The girl had to notice his hands. Huge, gnarled, rough. Sollie interrupted the scrutiny. "I'd like to look at su'thin' that'll plow snow."

"Oh — yes, of course," she said, and tripped across to whisper to a salesman. He came over, looking dubious, and said, "May I be of service?"

"Yes," said Sollie. "I need to plow a lot of snow."

"Yes, sir — will you step this way?"

He showed Sollie various machines, wondering the while what he had on his hands, and Sollie came back finally to the biggest item on the floor — a cleat tracker with big forward V-blade, two wings, and a complete hydraulic hoist. "I kind of like the looks of this," said Sollie.

"That's our most modern," said the salesman. "It's the largest tractor we have and extremely powerful. And rather expensive."

Sollie said, "Can you get that on a flatcar for Maine this afternoon?"

"Why, yes — I believe so. That is, well — have you spoken to our Mr. Smith?"

"Who's Mr. Smith?"

"He's our credit manager."

"What would I want to talk to him about?"

"Purely routine — you see, Mr. Smith arranges terms. We salesmen have nothing to say about the terms."

"Terms?" said Sollie. "Ain't money used in Bawst'n?"

So Sollie hauled out his wallet and counted $24,789 on the desk, and said, "I'll trouble you for a receipt."

"Yes, *sir!*" said the salesman. And the Jordan boys plowed snow for years, no matter how deep.

A Good Chance

A gentleman writes to me as follows:

Sir: I saw you'r book revued in the Yale Quarterly and sent four it to see if you had any good bare stories. I am sumthin of a bare man myself and have been intervued by noomerous professors on the subjeck. I think you're book is fare, but could stand som moar bare stories. If you would like I will speak onto a tape four you and give you som of my bare stories.

A Good Chance

Like how my grandmother hove a frying pan at a bare. She was a small woman so the story is told to point up how anybody can rise to an occasion. When eyeball to eyeball with a bare, a person has extry powers to resort to and this is what makes this bare story good. My grandmother was in the pantry one forenoon manufacturing som molasses cookies when she chanced to look up and see a bare standing besides her. Now, my grandmother wasn't the kind liked to have any interruptions when she was cooking so this kind of riled her and she reached around and grabbed up a cast iron frying pan off the shelf and she whopped that bare right on his nose. Then she whopped him again and that bare took off out the kitchen door into the yard and he headed for the woods off across the front field. My grandmother came out and saw him scooting off and she wound up and hove that frying pan after him. She didn't hit him, but that ain't the point. The point is, that she was so worked up over that bare that her system sprung into action and giv her extry power to meet the situashon. We went out and drove a stake where the frying pan came down and there ain't never been a man in our family could heav a baseball half that distance. It goes to show.

Another bare story you might use is how my grand-father was chaste one time by a she-bare and he hid in an empty rain barl. The bare backed up to the barl, looking all around for my grandfather, and quick as

scatt my grandfather reeched out through the bunghole and grabbed that bares tale and yanked it in through the hole and tied a not in it. Then he quick jumps out of the barl and the bare runs off with that rain barl on her behind, bumping her back leggs as she goes. It was kind of comical. Next spring my grandfather was plowing with the horses and he looks up and sees a string of baby bare cubs going along with kegs on there tales. This is a true story and I sware to it.

I think you need more bare stories and I'm your man.

> Very trully,
> (*signed*) Ted (Theodore) Raish

A Little Trip

Something of the way folklore develops in Maine is indicated by the chain reaction that came one February morning after Lottie Dunbar and Hilda Jameson had been talking on the telephone. It chanced that Mary Magoun listened in on the party line. It is a story that can't be rounded out to a full anecdote, because each segment has to be related as it happened. During the conversation Lottie said that she had her washing done.

A Little Trip

Mrs. Magoun thought she said, "We're going to Washington." As a consequence, for such is the practical application of the party line, it was but a short time before everybody in town knew that Lottie and Harold Dunbar were about to make a little trip.

Somebody said. "Why don't they wait and go in cherry blossom time?"

Since they were not waiting for cherry blossom time, there must be some other reason for the visit, so some speculated that Harold might have some business with the government and possibly was going to testify at a hearing. The more favored supposition was, though, that they were just going to see the sights and wanted to avoid the crowds that would be there when the cherries would be in bloom.

So nobody was at all surprised that afternoon when Mr. and Mrs. Dunbar rode by in their automobile. A few people who happened to be on the sidewalks waved farewell to them. As the gesture was a mite more exuberant than the usual uphand hi, Lottie and Harold responded in kind and waved back just as if they were off on a trip. Actually, they were merely going to Portland, where Harold owned a tenement building on Fore Street and went once every month to collect the rents.

Soon after they left, however, Mrs. Gertrude Launt looked across at the Dunbar residence and noticed that the garage doors were open. "My gracious," she said to herself. "They've gone and went on their trip and left their garage doors open!" She telephoned at once to Mrs. Amelia Williams and said, "Lottie and Harold have gone off and left their garage doors open!" The conclusion of the ladies was that in the excitement of departing the matter was an oversight, and that probably somebody should go and close the doors. Sometimes the worst storms of the season strike about now. They felt the proper thing was to notify the policeman and let him close the doors in legal form, and then he could keep an official eye on the place until the Dunbars should come home.

This was done. Merton Gail, the town constable, walked up and closed the doors and snapped the padlock on them. While he was there he tried the back door of the house, and he was surprised to find it unlocked. He twisted the inside knob, which set the lock, and closed the door. Very strange, he thought, that a man of Harold Dunbar's usual care would go off to Washington and leave everything wide open.

Mrs. Launt called Mrs. Williams again and said, "It's all right. I feel better now. Mert Gail just came up and closed the doors. My, if we'd had a storm I shouldn't have slept a wink."

It was, of course, fairly early in the afternoon when Harold and Lottie Dunbar returned from their drive to Portland and came into their dooryard to find the garage doors padlocked. "The key's in the kitchen drawer," said Harold. "I wonder who could have closed them?"

The next thing was to go down and get Tyler Cummings, the local jeweler and locksmith, who came and tried a whole big bunch of keys one by one until he found one that would unlock the Dunbar's back door. While doing this he said, "I thought you people went on a trip."

"We did," said Harold. "We went to Portland."

"No," said Tyler, "Washington — everybody was saying you went to Washington."

"Why would we go to Washington?"

"Well, the word was that you'd gone down to see the cherry blossoms."

"My goodness," said Lottie. "It's nowhere near time for cherry blossoms."

"All I know is what people tell me," said Tyler Cummings.

So the upshot was that in the days which followed, Mr. and Mrs. Dunbar chuckled to themselves about the way news can spread in a small town, and one evening Harold said, "You know — it's not such a bad idea at that. I've always wanted to see the cherry blossoms."

So they made arrangements, got a hotel room, and when it came cherry blossom time they went to Washington — previous to which Harold locked the back door and the garage and put the keys in the glove compartment of his automobile.

But when Carolyn Hinckley heard that Harold and Lottie Dunbar had left for Washington to see the cherry blossoms, she said, "For Heaven's sake, what's come over them? They was just down there in February!"

Among the Ladies

Years ago, in the days of hand-set type, Henry Upton was the foreman at the *Times* printshop in Bath, and he sent an order to the American Type Founders for twelve pounds of Century capital I's, long primer. This would make such a great quantity of the same letter that the American Type Founders questioned the order, and to assure them it was just what he wanted, he wrote back, "We are composing the autobiography of Roger T. Felding."

Roger T. Felding was one of these people who walk about looking like a retired Presbyterian clergyman who is probably passing his time writing Sunday School quarterlies. There was, really, nothing about him that anybody could find fault with, but nobody ever saw him pass without wondering. No scandal ever circulated about Roger T. Felding, and this is precisely why he entered local folklore. There was an autobiography of Roger T. Felding, and the *Times* Company did print it, and Mr. Felding was a man who saw no need of economizing with I's. He admitted graciously that he was the most important person in the world — if not in so many words, then in the manner in which he walked up the street. It was undoubtedly Henry Upton, although never proved, who elevated Roger T. Felding into the legends.

An early example of this appeared in a small social note in the *Times*, which was an afternoon daily. Well down in the column it said the South Street Ladies Guild had a tack at the home of Mrs. Damon Spears, followed by a collation. Among the ladies present, it said, were the fifteen or so who really were there, "and Roger T. Felding."

Mr. Felding was the only man in the city who was not amused, and he came to see Mr. F. B. Nichols, who was a good friend and owner of the *Times*. Mr. Nichols, who must have been somewhat amused, feigned anger and charged out in the back shop to demand who had perpetrated this thing. The boys feigned back, and to a man denied they had even seen the scurrilous error. Whereupon Mr. Nichols asked to see copy, and a great search was made to satisfy Roger T. Felding. In the end Mr. Nichols explained to him that in the rush of composition and makeup any handful of type could get mixed in somewhere, and this must be what had happened.

"Why," said Mr. Nichols, "I remember one time we got a birth in the obituary column, so you can see how these things happen." Mr. Felding seemed mollified, and that was that.

Then, in unexpected contexts and at no set frequency, the name of Roger T. Felding appeared in the *Times* for a long period of years. Mr. Nichols could always quiet him down, and since there was a long standing Nichols-Felding friendship nobody in the shop was too afraid of a lawsuit. At one time the sheriff raided a cockfight, and the list of respondents included Roger T. Felding. The last place anybody would ever find Mr. Felding would be at a cockfight, and the last thing that would ever happen to him would be an arrest for anything, and the readership chuckled. After a number of such inclusions, any one of which was solid grounds for the libelous "imputation of a crime," Mr. Nichols gave strict orders that no matter what he did, even if he died, the name of Mr. Roger T. Felding was not to be published in the *Times*.

He did not appear in the *Times* again for almost a year, when he was reported as carrying the flag in the Memorial Day parade. He had not even attended the exercises. Then he was listed as an usher at a wedding when he had not attended. The next year four men fell from a smelt shanty through the ice and died, and

Roger T. Felding was the fifth of the four. In all this time there was no proof as to who was working this. But as the community grew fonder of the whimsy, various readers would suggest to members of the *Times* staff that the name of Mr. Felding might be inserted here, or there, with pleasant outcome. And very often, in those little news notes that come to a local paper unsolicited, Mr. Felding would be found. The editor crossed him out of everything from a Boy Scout merit badge citation to the new members of the hospital staff. Even so, he frequently got in. Every busload of local fans that attended a Red Sox game at Fenway Park would include Roger T. Felding, who never went to sporting events, and one year when a similar group went to see the Bruins play hockey, Mr. Felding drove the bus.

Around town, it got so that folks included him in conversations. If you asked Charlie who was going duck hunting with him, he'd say Jim, Hank, and Mr. Felding. And one day a stranger came into the post office and said, "I'm wondering if you can help me with an address — I'm looking for Mr. Roger T. Felding." The burst of guffaws from the clerks in the office wasn't understood by the stranger, but anybody in Bath could have explained it.

One of the last appearances of Roger T. Felding in the *Times* came shortly before Henry Upton was transferred to the company's other printshop in Brunswick.

This may be evidence, and it may not. Some like to think it was Henry's last fling. Anyway, most of the Roger T. Felding appearances were pretty much in the same vein. The pianoforte pupils of Mrs. Katherine W. Busche would give a recital, and all the little children would have their names in the paper, and then it would say that Roger T. Felding played Rubinstein's "Melody in F." Like that. But for his swan song, if indeed 'twere he, Henry hit a noble climax.

The *Times* had just subscribed to the Associated Press service, and a loop came into the office. They now had national and foreign news to add to their front page, and they also had a closing stocks dispatch. The stocks would come over the wire just before press time, and there was little opportunity to give the copy and proof more than a glancing check. So there he was one afternoon, in his proper alphabetical place between Pan Am Petroleum and Rothschild Oil:

	OPEN	CLOSE	DOWN
Roger T. Felding	18½	18¼	¼

Good Answer

An old saying was that everybody in the town of Rangeley was either a Hinckley or a Hoar, and there were more Hoars than Hinckleys, because some of the Hinckleys . . . This was good humor rather than fact, for it protected the Haleys, another Rangeley family, who could just as well have been itemized for their ubiquity. The reason these family names predominated was that original settlers instituted them. The first Hoar came on snowshoes, dragging a handsled with his belongings, carrying a baby in his packsack, and looking back frequently to make sure his wife was keeping up. Anybody who could arrive in the Rangeley region in wintertime and establish a home was rugged enough to establish a healthy family, and it wasn't long before the countryside abounded in Hoars.

Along about the turn of the century one Gordon Hoar was prominent, and enjoyed the reputation of being the finest guide in the region. There were many people who wouldn't come to Rangeley to hunt and fish unless Gordon would guide them, and he seldom had a day off in open season. Not only was he woodswise but he was a captivating storyteller, and on stormy days he was worth his fee if he just sat around and yarned.

The scene now shifts, and we go to Boston. In those days Boston had a number of very fine grocery stores, one of which was operated by the firm of Cobb, Bates & Yerxa. Older Bostonians will recall this with a sigh, because this sort of grocery store has disappeared from the American scene. Even the great store of S.S. Pierce, the only one of its kind which lingers, has so changed its style and appearance, if not its stock, that comparisons are impossible. The Ginter Company, which extended its grocery business into restaurants, was one day to be absorbed by the Waldorf chain. The John T. Connor Company became the nucleus of the First National Stores — one of the earlier chains, and serving all of New England. And Cobb, Bates and Mr. Yerxa went their ways. An era ended. But around the turn of the century, when Gordon Hoar was guiding, Mr. Cobb came to Maine one early June with the thought of doing a little fishing. He went to Rangeley.

Fine grocery stores are not the only thing progress cast aside. Going from Boston to Rangeley was a joyous excursion. The details of such a trip are worth setting down. First, Mr. Cobb could ride from Boston's North Station in a deep-plush chair car, first class, over the Boston & Maine to Portland. At Portland he would not be obliged to change trains, but only to change cars. His porter would usher him from the chair car into an ordinary coach to the rear, and he would endure this low-grade accommodation for thirty-five minutes until he arrived at Brunswick. Maine was crisscrossed with branch railway lines in those days, and at Brunswick Mr. Cobb left the main line of the Maine Central Railroad and boarded the up train on the Lewiston-Rockland run. In another thirty minutes he was set off at a place called Crowley's Junction, a conductor having announced this station with a recital that only real old-timers can now recall: "Crowley's, Crowley's — Crowley's Junction, change for Leeds, Livermore, Jay, Wilton, and Farmington, please don't leave your packages in the car."

Mr. Cobb, being an affluent and important Boston Grocer, had baggage-checked any parcels he might have had, so he stepped down to the platform empty-handed and looked about. There wasn't much to see. The old Crowley farm across the fields and a few other homes at a distance. A depot and a few railway tool sheds. And on the other track, waiting for him, the train for Farmington. It left promptly, and Mr. Cobb observed that the scenery was comforting. Up past Sabattus Lake, through beautiful farming land, along the Androscoggin Lakes, and under the great looming piles of pulpwood at the Otis Mill in Chisholm. Shortly, from the train window, he had his first view of the incomparable skyline of Franklin County — range on range of mountains with only Canada beyond. Even though the train stopped at every village, the view from the window kept Mr. Cobb entranced, and he was surprised to be in Farmington so soon.

Railroading never had, anywhere else, what it was now about to offer Mr. Cobb. The Sandy River & Rangeley Lakes Railroad was a two-footer, a narrow-gauge operation entirely unique. It was a toy railroad complete in every detail. It had depots like any other railroad, with telegraph dispatch system, semaphores, and boards. Its conductors and trainmen wore uniforms, and most other narrow-gauge lines didn't attempt this refinement. As a subject for railroad historians and buffs it has no equal. Its roadbed was acknowledged the finest ever designed — for construction crews had only to dig where they were and they found bright glacial gravel exactly suited for their purpose. Trestles over the streams were no problem at all — logging crews cut huge spruce trees and laid them with the same skill they used for dams and sluices and lumber camps. Fuel was never a problem for the line — good Franklin County beech and maple were at hand, and the line never had to send to Pennsylvania for coal. To prevent forest fires a spark screen was fitted over the stacks. And most important of all, the S.R. & R.L.R.R. had the only Pullman car ever built for a two-footer railroad. Indeed, the car may be seen today, for after the little railroad went out of business up in Maine the car was taken to Carver, Massachusetts, where it is the pride of the Edaville Railroad, a museumlike enterprise in the cranberry zone. But when Mr. Cobb made his trip to Rangeley it was in honest use, and it was a revenue-maker for the Sandy River line. Hardly a "sport" came into the lake country but he paid extra to ride in the little Pullman, which was just as plush and just as comfy as anything on a cross-country run. Even more, because it rode the smooth gravel route, and cross-country lines never had such easy going.

Thus Mr. Cobb came to Rangeley, and a hack took him to the Lake House, where he was magnificently installed in their best room with a view, and the staff extended every hospitality. And after he was settled in, refreshed and rested from the trip, he spoke thus, "Will you arrange for a guide — I want to do some fishing."

This remark can be explained in two ways — either he didn't know the circumstances, or he felt his prominence as a fine Boston Grocer would produce miracles. Traditionally, people who come to fish at Rangeley make arrangements for their guides the previous season, or at least in the winter when dates may be open. However, pure chance accommodated Mr. Cobb. The desk clerk said, "I think you're lucky — we just had a party called back to Philadelphia unexpectedly, and I think a guide is available. Let me check."

So a bellhop was sent up to the guides' camp, and he

said to Gordon Hoar, "Gordie, they's a sport wants a guide." Thus it happened that the greatest guide in the Rangeley region met and guided the greatest grocer in Boston, and the introduction is never going to be forgotten.

"Mr. Cobb," said the desk clerk, "this is Gordon Hoar, your guide. Gordie, this is Mr. Cobb from Boston."

Mr. Cobb affably shook hands, as did Gordie, and with good humor Mr. Cobb said, "Hoar! That's an unusual name. I suppose you know what we do with them in Boston!"

"No I don't," said Gordie. "But I know what we do with cobs in Rangeley."

Coincidence

Coincidence is the strangest form of truth. No story-maker ever dreamed up anything, in his wildest fancy, that simple coincidence can't equal — the sheer im-probability that one thing will happen at the right time and the right place to jibe with something else nobody could have foretold. A couple of examples of Maine folklore will prove the point.

Back in the 1800's the Twenty Mule Team people

used to advertise their borax by driving a replica of
their Death Valley wagon around the country. Much
as the Anheuser-Busch breweries still use their Clydes-
dale horses. The borax entourage was not unlike a
small traveling carnival show, and it was billed
through an area by advance posters. Great crowds
turned out to see the big wagon go by, and as Maine
was still horse and oxen country there was special
interest in the hitch and the way it was handled. Actually, the twenty mules were only eighteen — the
hitch was led by two well-trained horses who responded to a twitch line and a whip crack. Possibly in
the wide open spaces of the borax country a sharp turn
by one of these hitches was seldom, but in holding a
borax parade through a city or town, every street
corner that had to be negotiated gave the spectators a
big thrill. If the animals had been turned when they
came to the corner, the wagon would run a closer circle
and end up on the sidewalk and against a building.
The trick was to run the animals out by until the
wagon was in the right position to make the corner,
then the driver would jump the horses and mules over
the traces, bring them around onto the new street, and
then have them start to pull again after they got back
over the traces. It was a maneuver that not one
teamster in ten thousand knew how to do, and the
driver of the borax cart was as great an artist as anybody. In the old days there were very few men who

could step up and say, "I can drive a twenty-mule team." And those who could were doing it.

So, one year in the glorious summertime the Twenty Mule Team came to Maine. It was due the next day in Gardiner, Hallowell, and Augusta, and it rested for the night in the small community of Whitefield. Whitefield, while there are those who love her, is off the beaten roads, sort of up back and in between, and hardly anything has ever happened in Whitefield. So when the mule team camped there for the night, excitement ran high. Garbed in Western costumes, the hostlers and attendants, the driver and cook, the advance man and the manager — all were closely inspected by the citizens of Whitefield, with special attention from the children. They were permitted to pat the mules and climb on the wagon, and it was great.

During the evening a message came for the driver of the Twenty Mule Team. It told him his wife had been in an accident in New York and had died. Everybody who had been visiting around the camp was sorry, of course, but the children of Whitefield lightened the sorrow with the thought that the mule team would stay there in town until the man had gone to New York, concluded his affairs, and could come back to drive away. The grieving driver left, and the manager began making arrangements to keep the camp right there. He made arrangements to get water and hay, and found rooms in some farmhouses for the various attendants. He felt the mules would be all right in the open, but he got the horses into a barn. And things settled in so it looked as if Whitefield would have the Twenty Mule Team for some time.

Then coincidence reared. From up on one of the hills of Whitefield came Maurice Endicott, a farmer now, but only lately returned from a young manhood in what Mainers called "The West." He had come home after years away to take over the family place. He approached the manager of the Twenty Mule Team.

"If you'd like," he said, "I'll drive the team, and we can keep the schedule going until the real driver comes back."

"That's decent of you," said the manager, "but it wouldn't work. It isn't everybody can handle the team. We'd have a good many more of these advertising wagons on the road if we could find men to drive them. Thanks just the same, but it isn't something I could just turn over to anybody. I can't even drive them myself."

"Were you ever in Death Valley?" asked Maurice Endicott.

"No, I'm just an advertising man out of New York."

"But you must know something about Death Valley and the borax business?"

"Well, yes — I've heard the stories, and I've studied the background."

"Did you ever hear anybody mention a driver out there by the name of Axel-Smoke Morrie?"

"Indeed I have. Axel-Smoke Morrie was the greatest mule-team driver of them all! He's legend!"

"Well," said Maurice Endicott, "I'm him."

So Maurice drove the mule team until the real driver came back, and although Whitefield missed the fun of having the caravan around for a time, everybody in town went over the next day to see Maurice Endicott turn the team into the Gardiner main street after he crossed the bridge from Randolph. It was something to see. And until that time nobody in Whitefield even guessed that Maurice Endicott was a genius.

The other Maine coincidence worth study concerns Eddie Maher and Stetson Plummer, who went hunting one fall up above Masardis. The region abounds in deer, but those who go after them run a risk of being snowed in. Having driven over bumpy woods roads, and often walked besides, hunters may wake some morning and find they can't drive out again. Stet and Eddie are excellent woodsmen, and they went pre-pared. They had plenty of food if they got storm-bound, and tire chains and shovels. Also snowshoes. So they arrived at the little camp they were to have — it was part of a logging cookshack that hadn't been moved out, and they got a permit from a paper com-pany. They started a fire in the stove, stowed their gear, cut branches for their beds, had a propitiating libation, and started supper. In the evening, by the oil lamp, they studied the geodetic survey maps to see where they would hunt in the morning. It was a wild, remote, uninhabited region, and they had it all to themselves. They decided they would hunt on the ridges across the river — if the river was frozen enough yet to let them cross.

When they set out the next morning, they came to the river in maybe half a mile, and they found that it was frozen. Stetson began to cross. Being good woodsmen, they tackled this properly. Eddie stood on the bank and watched, having a spruce pole ready to thrust at Stetson if the ice gave away, and after Stetson completed his passage he would do the same for Eddie. Suddenly the ice did break, and Stetson disappeared.

There is no way to describe this to anybody who hasn't had it happen. The heavy woolen clothing worn by hunters holds that marrow-freezing water away just long enough so the sensation, when it does reach you, is much improved. Stetson, alone under the water, had nobody to describe it to, and small desire to do so. He went down, and his toes touched bottom. He kicked, and the kick offset the current just enough so Stetson came up in the hole he had just gone down through. He had dropped his rifle, so he climbed to the ice and ran ashore. It happened to be the other shore. So Eddie was standing there horrified at seeing his friend disappear, but before he could reflex himself into motion to do anything, his friend was back up and over on the far bank. And they both knew the ice wasn't safe.

In this kind of a misfortune, the remedy is to get the wet clothes off, take something to start the heart and lungs again, and sit on a stove the rest of the day. Eddie and Stetson were therefore, in their minds' eyes, perusing again that geodetic survey map they had studied the night before. Eddie was a half-mile from camp, heat, and stimulants. Stetson, if he followed the river down to the Whitcher Bog road and then came back to camp, was at least eight miles from the same succor. This was because the river and the road took what is known as a devious course. But that was it, and there was only one thing to do.

"Run for it," yelled Eddie. "You run, and don't stop running. You run every step of the way, and don't for God's sake stop to rest. I'll stoke up the fire and get the camp warm. Now, start! And run!"

So Eddie watched Stetson take off down the far side of the river, and he knew it would be quite a time before Stetson would come to the road. Meantime, Eddie could stoke the fire and drive their pickup truck up the road to meet Stetson. "I just hope he can keep himself running," said Eddie to himself as he started back to camp.

There was no need to hurry, so Eddie didn't run. He

walked at a good pace, knowing he had ample time, and he opened the dampers on the stove, threw in some wood, and arranged a blanket on a chair so it would be hot-warm when Stetson needed it. He could now do nothing except drive the truck up to the Whitcher Bog bridge and wait for Stetson to come out of the woods. He opened the door of the camp to walk down to the truck, and just as he did a Yellow Cab drew up and Stetson got out of it.

But the thing about coincidence is that in its most incredible instances it is entirely plausible. Indeed, it is always so simple that any explanation may be construed as stealing the wind. True, while to Stetson there was now no miracle about his descending from a Yellow Cab, Eddie was pretty well shook up about it, and was a little put out that Stetson chattered his teeth so much the explanation was not understandable. It was, when he did hear it, so simple that he wondered why he hadn't figured it out.

The driver of the Yellow Cab was from Philadelphia, and he was a brother to the cook at the lumber camp in at Fifteen Mile Crossing. This camp was about to open for the winter chopping, and the brother made ready to come to Maine. The cab driver said, "I've never been to Maine, I'll drive you up." So on the day he was returning to Philadelphia, Stetson had decided to fall in the river, and as Stetson came out of the woods at the Whitcher Bog bridge a Yellow Cab went by and Stetson held up one finger and said, "Taxi!"

"Did he charge you anything?" asked Eddie.

"No. I offered to pay him, but he said his franchise was no good this side of New Jersey. But I gave him a dollar anyway. It was worth it. A wet dollar."

Pure Happenstance

Time has not yet advanced to give this next yarn folklore status, but it is an excellent example of coincidence and after a few more years may join the genre. It has to do with a Mr. James Hartley, former fire chief and now third selectman of the town of Raymond. Mr. Hartley is a fine old gentleman whose mind is still keen and alert about many things, and who is a delight to talk to. Evidently, from his stories, sheer chance has seen fit to insert him into unusual situations at the precise and proper time. Once, for instance, he told the Coast Guard where to go.

It was a foggy day, and he was off to the east'ard of Bailey Island in his boat. He wasn't lost, in a sense, but he wasn't just sure of his directions. He shut off his motor so he could listen for the breakers on the ledges, and was a little surprised that they came on his right hand and were not to the stern as he had expected. Just then he heard the thrum of an expensive marine engine, and knowing it was neither a fisherman nor summer mahogany, he peered in the fog toward the sound and saw the high prow of a Coast Guard cutter just above him. The vessel was barely under way, and there was hardly a ripple at the cutwater. Over the bow rail stared two Coast Guardsmen, their eyes fixed like four Long Green cucumbers, and one of them called down to Mr. Hartley and said, "Where are we? Which way to the open ocean?"

Mr. Hartley pointed an arm and said, "That-a-way!"

He chuckles to himself as he recalls the coincidence of his being exactly there, possibly the only person who ever told the Coast Guard where to go. But this small coincidence is nothing compared to the time he went fishing at Lost Loon Lake, far up in the Maine wilderness.

In those days he was a salesman for heavy railroad equipment. Since his only customers would be the purchasing agents for the major rail lines, his calls were long between. Just before he had left Cleveland, Ohio, on one trip a manufacturer said to him, "Why don't you see if you can't sell a few of our jacks. It's a new design for a hydraulic jack, and it will lift tremendous weights for its size." Jim said, "I think the best way to sell them is to have a few to demonstrate and deliver them in hand. Put some in the back of my station wagon." Of the dozen thus loaded in, Jim had sold six when he had finished with the Bangor & Aroostook Railroad on a certain Friday afternoon.

His next call would be in Rutland, Vermont, and the long weekend appealed to him as an excellent chance to relax and do a little trout fishing. So he made a couple of phone calls and got himself a pass over a logging company road and a cabin at Lost Loon Lake Camps. He drove far beyond the end of the state highway system, deep into the wilderness, and for the last forty miles he saw no other vehicle and no sign of people until he came to Lost Loon. Here he had a wonderful time, caught some trout, relaxed, and started off again on the Monday morning.

About halfway out over the long, winding logging road he came around a bend and found a lumber truck, loaded with pine sawlogs, parked. The two men with the truck were looking at a flat tire, and seemed astonished to see Jim pull to a stop. "We didn't expect to see anybody all day!" one of them said.

"Can I be of any help?" asked Jim.

Any student of the literary coincidence can easily supply the next line. The one thing that the two men with the truck would want has got to be the most unlikely thing for any chance passerby to have in a station wagon. The line goes:

"Not unless you got a twenty-ton jack, you can't."

"It just so happens," said Jim, "that I have."

He motioned over his shoulder and the two men looked in the back. One of them said, "Migawd, he's got six of them!"

What you've got to do, if you analyze this for folk-lore consideration, is figure out how that manufacturer in Cleveland knew Jim Hartley would decide to go fishing at Lost Loon Lake. That's all.

Malaga and Shiloh

Two folklorish topics in Maine history have had their facts embellished greatly, and at the same time have been obscured by a reluctance to speak up. They have no connection, except in the way their details have been handled, and they are both good examples of the way truth may be frugalized. One is Malaga Island and the other is Shiloh.

Some years ago a man from a big city newspaper wanted to do a story about Malaga Island, and he applied at the state library, maintained by the state in the statehouse, to look at their material — which included legislative records. From the first, he detected a reluctance, and afterwards they came right out and said that they didn't admire to have any publicity on this matter. The library staff of the time (not the present one) felt it would be prudent not to let the great world know about this seamy side of Maine's maritime affairs, and they gave the man a hard time. There isn't much about Malaga Island that can't be told quickly, to make an unpretty story short, and it is definitely in the record, so should not be withheld from the scholar. Furthermore, for the new days of integration, urban renewal, city planning, and social uplift, the Malaga Island affair was ahead of its time and offers great lessons as a pilot experiment.

Malaga Island is less than a square mile in area and sits off the mainland of the town of Phippsburg, which owns it. In the ancient days of sail, vessels constantly passed it, going and coming. And the legend runs that when Maine was embarking on its heroic history of world-round commerce, an occasional skipper of the ships, barks, brigs and luggers would, while in a far place, hanker and anhunger and even covet, and he would carry a seaside bride of convenience over the threshold of his cabin and make merry with her after the accepted fashion. This cheated the long weeks and months of a voyage and gave him something to do besides twiddle his thumbs, and all would be gay and pleasant until one morning he would arise from his bed of joy and look through his glass and see the spruce-lined coast of Maine. Here, alas, he had a wife and family and a happy home with a widow's walk where his true and lawful was pacing with eager heart to observe his return. All at once the comely lass in his cabin was superfluous.

Now, the lore continues, it was his custom to say, "My sweetest honey dear, we are about to arrive in a strange and fearful land where you would suffer numerous indignities. I do not care to subject my lamby-pie to such. So pack your things, and here is some money, and I will set you ashore on this lovely isle where you may await my return. On the way out I will pick you up, and we may continue our conversations."

So he did, but on the way out, he didn't. On the way out, which might be as much as a year later, he would hug the far shore of the channel and look the other way. Lovers' vows are writ on water. In time, since the average coastal Maine man has never been lackadaisical about his pursuit of some kinds of happiness, this lovely isle, which was Malaga, was well populated with wenches. They were, since down-east tastes proved catholic, of every breed and flavor known. Too, new recruits were arriving with every tide, and since each lady thus arriving was abruptly denied that which had heretofore been her sole function, there existed on the isle a great general yearning which made it a little dangerous for a man to approach. However, certain

fishermen and beachcombers managed to muster sufficient bravery and moved on. Some remained as perma-
nent residents, willing to suffer constantly, while
others came and went in occasional gentlemanly efforts
to assuage the deficiency which prevailed. As you may
properly surmise, Malaga Island became a mess.

About the turn of the century, after Maine's maritime glory waned, something had to be done, so a state
commission was named and action taken. It was fairly
forthright and might well be studied by modern agen-
cies which have similar tasks. The population of
Malaga Island was arbitrarily separated into families.
Since nobody had the faintest idea what, on Malaga
Island, a family might be, the procedure was to take a
man, a woman, and whatever children seemed most
likely to fit, and as if an expanded wedding ceremony
were being performed, to say, "Behold! You are now a
family!" Then, family by family, the Malaga Island-
ites (as they were called) were settled in communities
up and down the coast and each town thus favored was
required to support them if need be.

More might be made of it, but essentially that's
about what it amounted to, and all of it is in the
legislative records. It worked out rather well. Even
today some Maine towns know just which of its people
derived from Malaga Island, and here and there a successful and prominent citizen proves that the lowly
may ascend. Now and then some summer visitor may

notice olive skin, half-slanted eyes, kinky hair — and wonder. But an old-time Mainer would say, "Malaga Island."

The Shiloh story is something else again, although equally hidden in reluctant fog. Frank Sandford was a college man and a baseball player, also a persuasive and articulate minister of the gospel. His personality in the pulpit was full as good as that of Billy Sunday and Dwight Moody. His theological ambition was to found a holy community where God would constantly be praised and happy people would share the bounties of prosperity. He acquired a sandy hilltop in the town of Durham, and here he gathered his followers to live in communal joy and sing the good old hymns. A great many people came from far places to join him. So many, indeed, that a huge complex of buildings was erected that easily equaled the old Poland Spring Hotel. The temple with its golden dome and gilded stairway was on one corner of the vast quadrangle, with separate buildings beyond for the school and the hospital. The community was so large that the postal service gave it its own office. The establishment atop "Beulah Hill" could be seen from miles away, and the golden dome of the temple and the tall "praying towers" gave the place great magnificence.

The religion of Frank Sandford was simple and fundamentalist. It was the Word of God, but it encompassed many philosophic nuances of merit. Even today, long after Sandford is gone and the heyday is over, it continues to satisfy many, and Beulah Hill still has its faithful. The vast buildings have been reduced until only the temple itself remains. It still has its gilt, and the Sunday services in it are open to the public. The curious who join the Shilohites find it little more than another Sunday worship, hardly atune with the folklore that has been added to the fact.

It was not the theology, but the communal problems that brought woe to Sandford's dream. Surging as Elijah, if not a messiah, he reached beyond his practical grasp. There were times when the colony was desperately hungry and had no answer except to pray. One of their philosophic nuances was that the sun should never be allowed to set upon a debt, so they could not ask for credit — nor would they have gained any had they asked. When their prayers were answered and some money showed up, they would send a wagon after food, and if God's kindness struck them at three o'clock in the morning they would arrive at that hour to rouse up the grocer. The old Harding store in Lisbon, across the river from Durham, was owned by Hardings who disliked such interruptions, so they put a special outside lock on their warehouse and gave Frank Sandford the key. After that the Shilohites would come and fetch their staples whenever God answered their orisons, and the Hardings stayed abed. And without fail, somebody came from the colony before the next sundown to pay the tab. Those who berated the Shilohites the most could never impugn their honesty.

Sandford weathered many a crisis, and endured constant belittling and even persecution, but his downfall came with his ambitious crusade to the Holy Land. Our great Maine poet and chronicler, Robert P. Tristram Coffin, erred greatly in his treatment of this. He described the fervor of the thousands of hymn-singing faithful who lined the decks as the vessel departed. But the Sandford boat was small and could carry only a few. Thus the Shiloh story was usually misreported. That people did starve and that scurvy did erupt, that conditions were bad, and that Sandford wasn't much of a sailor and navigator — these things are undoubted. But public indignation was fed by sensationalized news stories, and the law moved in and preferred charges. The law could not take notice of the zeal, fervor, and devotion of Sandford's people, so the outcome was predictable. Sandford was jailed and the great era on Beulah Hill was over. The Shiloh post office was discontinued.

Sandford's public image, by the time the courts and the newspapers got through with him, was little more than that of a premeditating murderer — a distortion by the bigotry and persecution for which mankind has an aptitude. There was, if anyone had really cared, extenuation, excuse, and explanation. Some, anyway.

But the sordid "revelations" caused the devout Shilohites to draw into themselves even more, and since then they have resented intrusion and resisted and discouraged the curious. Nobody knows how many times students in our Maine colleges have redone the Shiloh story as a major thesis and how many have wended up Beulah Hill with scholarly intent, to be rebuffed at the gate with, "We prefer to be left alone — but you will be welcome at Sunday services." If the student combs the newspaper files to learn about Shiloh, he finds a day-to-day account which contains little more truth than the thesis he will himself compose. He will find recitations of "alleged" sufferings and atrocities. And Sandford never appears to be what he truly was — a dedicated dreamer who awoke, one day, to reality. Shiloh means, "a place of rest." There was also a long rest in the penitentiary.

But the abbreviated Shiloh still stands on Beulah Hill, and something of Sandford's influence must be read in the quiet reverence that orders the lives of those who still hear his words. If they get something at the store, they come before sunset to square their accounts. It is difficult to find honest fault with that part of Sandford's theology.

So the Malaga Island story and the Shiloh story persist in our interest, and the peripheral saga that surrounds each may be entered in the record. But oftentimes one wonders if the former state librarian mightn't have had a point — perhaps it would be well to pass by on the other side.

Went to Sea

"It *is* an unusual place for a tombstone, but nobody's buried under it. It's Henry Bodwell's. They put the stone up the summer after he died, and after he went to sea. You never heard that story? Well . . .

"It was in my father's time. This Henry Bodwell was quite a rooster. He built bridges and dams for the logging companies, and did some guiding in the summer, and he was quite a hand with the ladies. He managed to sidestep until he was about sixty-five, and then he got caught up with a gay summer widow who showed up at the Lake House. He guided her some. So when the season was over this widow took a camp at Upper Dam and had it fixed up so she could spend the winter, and she was going to stay. She was an artist or a writer, or some crazy thing like that, and as everybody figured she and Henry had tangled already, nobody was much surprised when Henry moved in with her. He spent the winter there with her, and when they came to town in the spring to grocery up you never saw such a change. She came bouncing along as if she had the world by the tail on a downhill cant, and poor Henry came dragging along like a hound that has managed to survive the distemper. He looked like a fish drifting downstream tail first.

"And by gorry, Henry died. Along on the downhill side of March he just drifted off into his eternal sleep. Everybody in town knew what killed him, and most people said it was a lovely way to go. There's no law against that kind of a murder weapon, and Henry had asked for it. My father was one of the bearers, and he said Henry had a fine funeral. Said when they picked the coffin up Henry didn't weigh hardly anything. Just skin and bones. And he'd never had a sick day in his life.

"Now, this widow woman he'd been comforting was just as sorrowful as if they'd been matrimonialized, and she carried on and made a big fuss. Said she wanted her Henry to be buried over at Upper Dam, where memories were so pleasant. It wasn't a bad idea, my father said, because the place was sandy and they could dig it. Back in town there was still frost and plenty of snow, but along the river the sun had done some work. So they dug, and they laid Henry to rest.

"Well, it came off to two days of fog, and then it rained hot water all one night, and winter was over. The lake commenced to rise, and so did the rivers, and where Henry had just been laid in and his coffin was full of air, darned if he didn't pop right up out of the ground and float away. The widow woman saw it, but there was nothing she could do, and by the time she got some help Henry was long gone. They looked for him. They cruised Upper Richardson, and then Lower Richardson, and in the next few days they did all the lakes, but about the time they were ready to give up, word came that Henry had just gone over the falls at Rumford. He'd sailed right through the lakes, and gone down the Androscoggin River. They said his coffin went over the falls like an Indian canoe.

"In the next few days they tried to catch him along the river. But he didn't eddy up or beach out, and when he was sighted it was mostly in white water where nobody dared to go out and tow him ashore. Couldn't seem to catch him at a quiet time. They saw him at Livermore Falls and again at Lewiston. They tried to snag him at Brunswick, where they had people lined up on the Swing Bridge with gaffs, but they missed him and while they were still watching, the word came that he was just off the Bath Iron Works. They said every boat they could get was out combing the lower Kennebec for him, but people figured he must have crossed into the Sassanoa and gone out to sea that way. They never sighted him again.

"The stonecutter had gone right to work, of course, and he had a monument finished before Henry set out.

They didn't know just what to do with it, so they put it here. Good a place as any, I suppose. My father said there was some talk of adding one line — "Lost at Sea" — but too many people thought that would be a mite frivolous under what was really sad circumstances."

Several Champions

"Champion swearer in my memory was the cook at Rainey Brook lumber camp the year we built the dam. He was good. Not only had a great command of words but his diction was clear as a bell and he had a voice to go with it. Had a way of chanting, like a priest singing mass, sort of — but not quite. He could go on and on and surprise you with new words after you thought he'd said them all. Most effective. I remember one morning he dropped a pot of hot coffee on his leg and he started to swear, and it was so rugged that seventeen of my best choppers were obliged to leave the table."

"We had the world's greatest insurance salesman in Caribou. He sold so much insurance he was written up in all the trade papers, and one year they invited him to come to New York and tell the national convention how he did it. He made up a fine speech and tried it out on some of the people around Caribou, and it was good. They had thirty-five hundred of the best insurance salesmen in the country up in the big banquet hall on the top floor of the hotel, and they all sat there waiting to hear the secret of our man's success. But, you know, they waited and waited, and he didn't come. Finally they decided to call it off and adjourn, when in he comes — full of business and his briefcase up under his arm, and he rushes up to the speaker's stand and starts right in talking. "Awful sorry to be late," he says, "but I've been riding up and down for the last hour — that elevator boy was hard to sell."

"No — nobody goes for eels in this pond. Don't dare. I know. Way we used to go eeling was take a skiff at night and set a lighted lantern in it. Then we'd fish over the side with an eel bob and slat them into the skiff. Was nothing to go home with the skiff half full of eels. Used to make an eel bob with Aunt Liddy thread, running it through big, fat worms with a needle. Then catch it up into a loose ball. Idea is that an eel's teeth hang like a woodchuck's, and once he grabs on he can't get away as long as you keep the line tight. When he comes in over the side of the boat you ease off, and he drops. Saves digging out hooks, and if you know how

an eel takes in a hook you'll see the sense of an eel bob.
Anyway, about the eels in this pond here — they're
the biggest eels in the world. One time my brother and
I fished here, when we were boys, and he got an eel
that I'd say was about medium size for this pond. He
hauled him in, and when he fell off the bob the boat
sank."

"Strongest man I ever knew was a Frenchman. Built
close to the ground, and legs on him like spruce
stumps. One time Mose Shively and Harry Starbird
were loading logs, and they had one sixteen-footer that
would go about an ax handle at the butt, and it set off
by itself so they had to move it out to the load. They
were rigging poles to cant her when this Frenchman
came along, and he says, 'Boys, I don't think you need
to dog her. I'm here — why don't we just pick her up
and lug her over?' So Mose links his arms around one
end, and Harry does the same on the other, and this
Frenchman tackles her in the middle. Up she came,
and Harry and Mose had their eyes bugged out and it
was all they wanted to do to stay with it. Well, to show
you how strong he was, they came to a cradle knoll so
the Frenchman had to walk over it, and there he was
with the log, and Harry and Mose was right up off the
ground with their feet pawing the air. Quite a strong
man."

"He warn't what I'd call a lavish feeder. His stock was always poorly. Probably the meanest man with a hayfork that ever lived. Why, he had a flock of pigs in his front field, and they were so thin you couldn't see them unless they were side to."

"Well, size is all according to. Some things is long at six inches, and some things is short at two miles. It depends. It's like my aunt with her knitting machine. I suppose you're too young to remember them knitting machines? There'd be an ad in the magazine that said, 'Earn Money at Home!' and if you answered it they'd send you a knitting machine and a bale of yarn. The one my aunt had would knit socks. Just turn the crank and feed in the yarn and out would come socks. She picked up quite a bit of money cranking the thing an hour or so a day. It was screwed to the wall in the back entry, and I don't know what possessed us, but we boys commenced cranking on it, and where we didn't know how to turn the heel we kept cranking, and we knit a sock that was a hundred and eighty-eight feet long. That's a good length for a sock. I always wondered what become of it. I never knew, because after my aunt just about cut my legs off with a switch she sent me home."

"Henry ain't really a minister — he's a memorizer. You let him read something over, and he can repeat it word for word. Never looks at notes when he's in the pulpit. No, he didn't go to Bible school, he got his training over at Goodey's store at Leeds. Well, Goodey had one of these eyeglasses cabinets — this was away back before they had eye doctors. All the different eyeglasses were in little drawers, and if you needed glasses you'd go in and try them on until you found one that seemed to help. Goodey had a Bible there to look at while you were trying them on. So Henry used to go in and make believe he was trying on glasses, and what he was doing was memorizing the Bible. Made him the best damn preacher we ever had around here. Never had a thing the matter with his eyes."

"Nellie Grant could have been the oldest woman in the state. Well, when she was a hundred the whole town turned out to pay respects, and during the party somebody tipped over an oil lamp. Poor Nellie was sitting there in a soft rocker with a shawl around her and all her presents piled up, and all at once there was this flash and she was surrounded by flame. Didn't do any damage and they slapped the fire out right away, but for anybody her age it gave her an awful start. Scared at least ten years right off her life."

"I wasn't built hefty and I never could pick up much in the way of weight. But so long as it wasn't heavy, I could pick up bulky things and go with them all day.

When we stocked the lumber camp at Round Pond I carried in a good part of the stuff. I remember one load I took right in over Hedgehog Mountain — seventeen mattresses and a hundred and sixty-seven tin dippers with no handles on."

"The greatest striptease show anybody ever saw was in the church at West Bowdoin. Right in the pulpit. It's true. Sunday morning, at that. I was just a tyke, and we had quite a time getting to church that morning on account of a new snowstorm. But quite a congregation made it, and we were all in our pews before the minister came. He was from Bowdoinham and used to supply. I guess his old horse had a time of it bellying through those drifts, but finally he made it, and he whipped right into the church and on up to the pulpit because he was late. He hauled off his mittens and his hat, and put them on a chair, and then he unwinds a big muffler. After that he peeled off his overcoat, and by now he was through the prayer and was starting on the sermon. Under his overcoat he had a leather jerkin, and he takes that off. Then he has a sweater. Finally he gets down to his regular suit of clothes, and by this time he is all wrapped up in his message and praising the Lord with great effect, and I guess he got carried away because he takes off his pants. I suppose it was quite a natural thing to do. I'll never forget it."

Smart Dog

"You never knew Herb Spinney over to Maquoit. Before your time. He was the unluckiest man in Maine. Well, before he was born his ma and pa had a baby boy that they named Hubert. Hubert died when he was four or five. And the stone cutter made a mistake. Instead of putting Hubert Spinney on the stone he put Herbert Spinney. Had to make another one, of course, but here was this stone with Herbert already cut on it, and there wasn't any Herbert Spinney. So when Hubert's pa and ma had another baby boy born to them they didn't see any sense in wasting a tombstone, so they named the new little fellow Herbert. It isn't everybody has his gravestone cut before he's born. All his life Herbert had his tombstone upstairs in his barn, all ready to go. Kind of an odd thing to live with, but you can see how it happened. Unlucky? Oh, yes — I said he was unlucky. Well, he was. Never got a chance to use his own tombstone — he was lost at sea."

Smart Dog

Clevie Bickford came into Phil Allen's feed store one spring and said, "My dog died, and I'm going to plant a piece of sweet corn."

"I'm sorry to hear that," said Phil. "He was a smart little fellow — but what does that have to do with sweet corn?"

"I don't wonder you ask," said Clevie, "but it's got everything to do. He was probably as smart as any dog I ever had, and I guess that was his trouble. He was like a lot of people I know — they're smart, but they have things figured out wrong.

"Now, that dog would do anything I asked him to. Show him something once, and he had it. And one year just as my patch of sweet corn was coming in, a flock of squirrels came out of the woods and began working it. All at once I found ears stripped down, and I could see the squirrels. So I called my dog, and I showed him the squirrels, and I showed him the ears of corn stripped down, and I told him I didn't want the squirrels bothering the corn — and I knew that would take care of that. He understood me, and I never had to show him anything twice. He barked and wagged, and went over and barked at the squirrels, and I could see the matter was well in hand.

"Well, sir — it was, and it wasn't. That dog took over, but he had got the message twisted. Instead of keeping the squirrels away, he thought I was teaching him to eat sweet corn. Cleaned out the whole patch that afternoon, and buried cobs all over the farm. So, as long as I had him, I couldn't grow sweet corn. But he died, and I want five pounds of Golden Bantam seed."

Secession Incident

President Abraham Lincoln got himself considerable notoriety by quelling the rebellion, better known as saving the Union, but the historians have nothing to say about the rebellion he didn't quell, and the secession that succeeded. It's an old Maine tale variously told, and about Loud's Island. Loud's Island, more properly called Loudville, seceded from the Union in 1861 along with eleven Confederate States. After the war the others came back, but Loud's Island is still seceded.

The present-day folklorist needs to understand the situation at that time. There had long been prosperity on the Maine coast. It began before Columbus was born, when salt cod tasted good in Europe. It roused into the great era of sail, when Maine built ships, manned them, and traded the goods of the world. This was at its peak just before the Civil War.

Many a Maine offshore island which is today a haven of solitude for "summer complaints," or the

home of a few lobstermen, was in those days a thriving
community. People stood with their backs to the mainland — which was "the main," or Maine — and had
their eyes on the sea. They didn't come ashore to travel
overland; if they went anywhere it was by boat. Their
mail came by boat. Their horizon was busy with sails.
The ocean was their highway and their living.

The war not only brought an end to this, it doomed
living on islands. All along the Maine coast you'll find
island rosebushes, lilacs, grapevines, and cellar holes.
An occasional house was saved for a summer place by
somebody with wealth and leisure, and a few more
have been kept by fishermen. Loud's Island was such
an island, and is such an island. It is a beautiful place.

Another matter folklorists, and historians, must remember is that Maine was not sold on that war. Too
much cotton moved in Maine vessels. It is true that no
other state sent such a proportion of her manpower to
fight for Father Abraham, but it is also true that
Maine people demonstrated and rioted, many "paid
off" the draft, and some skedaddled. Away up on
Kennebago Lake, in what is still wilderness, there is a
place called Skedaddlers' Cove — men who opposed
the war struck out and disappeared, and some few
went as far as Kennebago. This was not new — in
Revolutionary times many Mainers with sympathy for
the Crown did the same, and in Saint John, New
Brunswick, you can find tombstones to attest that they

never came back. Draft dodging is not peculiar to the twentieth century. And all in all, it is perfectly understandable that the men of Loud's Island were not eager to march off and free the slaves. They ignored the draft call and kept a-fishing.

The island seceded from the Union. They weren't interested, and they wanted to be left alone. The only difference between them and the Confederacy is that the Confederacy came back into the fold after the war, and Loud's Island stayed seceded.

Washington, D.C., may not acknowledge this fully, but there is good evidence to support it. In 1946 Stanley B. Attwood published a book called *The Length and Breadth of Maine*. It is the best authority. It exhausts everything in the way of geography, flora and fauna, place names, variations in spellings, surveys, and such. It is meticulous in all respects. It not only lists townships, but sections of each. And in this book, while he covers all else completely, Mr. Attwood curiously neglects Loud's Island. His two references are brief and incomplete. One is: "Loudville. Discontinued PO in BRISTOL." The other simply lists Loudville as being part of Bristol. Nothing is said about its being an island, and he does not give latitude and longitude — as he does with all other islands. Yet "Jones Garden" is carefully listed by Mr. Attwood. Jones Garden is nothing but a rock, uninhabited and uninhabitable, a perch for seagulls and a navigational hazard in Muscongus Bay. The word "garden" as applied to the rock is meant to be contemptuous, or at least funny, in respect to the farming skills of the Jones family. It is strange that Mr. Attwood so thoroughly treats Jones Garden, which lies off Loudville to the east'ard, but passes over the much larger and more consequential Loud's Island.

Yet it is not strange at all. Loud's Island seceded. She doesn't belong.

There was an effort to bring the Loud's Islanders to heel. It was a small military expedition and ill-fated. Whether or not President Lincoln personally ordered it is not known, but on a warm spring day a rowboat pushed out from Round Pond and headed for Loud's. A draft sergeant, accompanied by a squad of men, was about to reduce the rebellion. It must have been just such a tableau as Washington's crossing of the Delaware.

If a city on a hill cannot be hid, it is equally true that a Maine island is hard to approach by stealth. Even at night in thick o' fog people somehow know you're coming. On a bright morning there was no secret about the boat's coming from Round Pond. So when the draft sergeant and his squad pulled in at Prior's Cove the menfolks of Loud's Island were long gone. They had up-sailed and awayed, and were far past Monhegan on their way to the Banks. The draft sergeant and his squad found only women and children on Loud's Island.

But they made a thorough search, and in a secluded spruce grove they came upon a small cottage that overlooked the surging shore. Smoke rising from the chimney indicated occupancy, and they moved in with caution. The sergeant ordered his men to stand at the ready, and in consequence of the powers vested in him by the Commander in Chief he kicked open the door.

This surprised an old granny who lived there alone and didn't know what was going on, and at the moment she was stooped over the fireplace hearth, turning a potato she was baking for her dinner. This sudden show of the military frightened her into defense, so she scooped up the hot potato and let it fly.

The sergeant, flanked by his men with muskets in hand, had the disadvantage of being in the bright sunlight while peering into the dim cottage, whereas Granny had the element of surprise on her side. Too late, the sergeant ducked, and the potato caught him full on the side of his head, where it burst with that mealy consistency possessed by a good Maine potato and filled his ear channel with grievous, hot, excruciating pain. The war was over.

He jumped around some, and his men tried to run him down before he could jump off a cliff, and after about six good bounds he was back at Prior's Cove and the expedition was pulling oars for Round Pond.

There was no further effort to nullify the secession. Loud's Island stayed seceded. Granny had to bake another potato, and while it was coming along she hurried over to the nearest house to find out what had happened, anyway. It would be fun to report that Granny's name was Lee, but it wasn't. It was Simmons.

An Old Story

A wisp of Maine coastal lore that needs to go into the record concerns the proper way to immerse a live lobster in boiling water — a culinary matter. Visitors to Maine who have never before seen this done always shudder at the sight, and there is one story of a lady who felt it was so cruel that she couldn't bring herself to do it — but always put the lobster in cold water and then brought it to a boil.

But the wisp itself: When a summer lady asked, "But isn't that extremely painful to the lobsters?" the Maine housewife replied, "Oh, no — they're used to it."

Couldn't Read It

Speaking of grindstones, there used to be an old duffer ran a little store up at Seboomook Landing, which in those days was about as far away from anything as you could get. You've got to realize that a "store" in that great wilderness region wouldn't be much like one any place else. It was rather more of an old trading post, and its stock was meant to be helpful to the woodsmen around about.

Myron Titcomb, who owned the store and was its only clerk, had never enjoyed the luxury of formal schooling, and kept his books after the cuneiform system. Whenever anybody charged anything, Myron would go over and get down his big journal book and draw pictures in it. It worked fine. A man would come in to pay what he owed, and Myron would get down the book. There would be a picture of an ax, a pouch of tobacco, some muskrat traps, and so on, and as fast as an account was cleaned up Myron would scribble on the pictures to indicate they were paid for.

One day in the late fall of 1887 a gentleman from Cambridge, Massachusetts, paused at Myron's store on his way through from a hunting trip, and somehow he chanced to get away without paying. Just oversight. Myron didn't know who he was or where he was from, but he got his book down and made his pictures — thinking by good luck the man might some day come through again.

And the man did. In the spring of 1910 he came up to do some fishing, and by this time he had just about forgotten that he was ever there before. But as he came into the store he said, "My, my — I recall this place!"

Myron looked up and recognized him.

"Yep," said Myron. "You was here in November of 1887."

"That's right, I was," said the man. "How in the world do you have such a precise memory?"

"Because you didn't pay me when you was here."

"I didn't?"

"Nope."

"Well, I certainly don't remember, one way or the other. How did it happen?"

"You just forgot, I guess, and was gone before I could tell you."

"So I owe you some money?"

"Yep."

"What would it be for?"

"Twelve grindstones."

"Ha, ha," said the man. "I get it. What's the joke?"

"No joke — you owe me for twelve grindstones."

"Now come on," said the man. "I was ready to believe perhaps I'd forgotten to pay, but not for anything like that. I never owned a grindstone, let alone more than one. What would I do with twelve grindstones?"

"My God, Myron," said Mel Smith, who was standing listening to all this, "I believe he's got you. You never sold twelve grindstones in your whole life, let alone to one man. Reason's on his side. What are you trying to pull?"

"Nawthin. I got him down in the book, and he's owed me since 1887. I was going over the accounts last night, and I see it."

"Let me see," said the man.

So Myron got the book down and when he found the place he turned it on the counter so the man could see, and there was the entry:

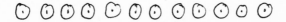

"Twelve grindstones," said Myron. "Clear as a bell."

"Let me look at that," said Mel Smith.

"Twelve grindstones," said Myron.

Mel said, "Myron, you're a damn fool. You can't even read your own writing! That's not twelve grindstones."

"It looks like twelve grindstones to me," said Myron.

"Well, it ain't. It's a dozen doughnuts!"

Acknowledgments

The State of Maine must lead off on an acknowledgment page, and all who live there — but most of these yarns have multiple sources. I do not recall if Alden Grant or Dean Fisher first told me of the twelve grindstones — I lean toward Grant, but Fisher may think otherwise. The story appeared in the *Christian Science Monitor* on May 1, 1969, and is retold here with permission. Everybody deserving thanks is hereby thanked, and a special thank-you to Mrs. Glenys Thompson, clerk of the town of Lisbon, who lent me the municipally owned numbering stamp, without which I should have been obliged to number the manuscript sheets by hand. This was a great help.

JOHN GOULD

Lisbon Falls, Maine